CAVENDISH
LawCards

European Community Law

Cavendish
Publishing
Limited

First published in Great Britain 1997 by Cavendish Publishing Limited, The Glass House, Wharton Street, London WC1X 9PX, United Kingdom.

Telephone: +44 (0) 171 278 8000

Facsimile: +44 (0) 171 278 8080

e-mail: info@cavendishpublishing.com

Visit our Home Page on http://www.cavendishpublishing.com

© Cavendish Publishing Limited 1997

Reprinted 1997, 1998

All rights reserved. No part of this publication may be reproduced, stored in a retrieval system, or transmitted in any form or by any means, electronic, mechanical, photocopying, recording or otherwise, without the prior permission of the publisher.

Any person who infringes the above in relation to this publication may be liable to criminal prosecution and civil claims for damages.

Lawcard on EC law

1.European Community - Law and legislation 2.European Community - Law and legislation - Examinations, questions etc. 3. Law - Europe 4. Law - Europe - Examinations, questions etc.

I.EC law

341.2'422

ISBN 1 85941 329 3

Printed and bound in Great Britain

Contents

1   Sources of law

Sources of law

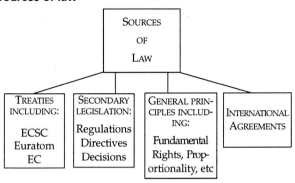

There are three sources of EU law:

- law enacted by the EC (secondary legislation) or the Member States (primary legislation);

- general principles of law recognised by the European Court of Justice;

- international agreements with non-Member States.

Primary legislation

One of the main characteristics of the EU legal order is that it is based on a written constitution. The constitutive Treaties are, as follows:

- ECSC Treaty;

- EC Treaty;

- EURATOM Treaty;

- Convention on Certain Institutions Common to European Communities;

- Merger Treaty;

- First and Second Budgetary Treaties;

- Treaties of Accession;

- Single European Act;

- Treaty on European Union.

European Coal and Steel Community Treaty (ECSC)

Established by the Treaty of Paris in 1951, the purpose of the European Coal and Steel Community is to create a common market for coal and steel products.

The ECSC Treaty was the first of the constitutive Treaties. It exhibits a functionalist approach to integration, which attempts to integrate economies sector by sector. A criticism of this approach is that it is an unnatural operation as the integrated sector retains indissoluble links with the other sectors of the economy which still have their national character. Its justification is that it is a first step and is to be followed by integration of other sectors of the economy until the whole economy is eventually integrated.

An innovative feature of the ECSC Treaty was the creation of four supra-national institutions:

- Council of Ministers – representing the Member States;

- High Authority – intended as a supra-national executive consisting of independent individuals rather than government representatives, empowered to take legally binding decisions and to procure funds, fix maximum and minimum prices for certain products and fine businesses in breach of competition rules;

- Assembly – a parliament composed of delegates appointed by respective Parliaments of the Member States;

- Court of Justice – to review the legality of the Acts of the High Authority, or in some cases, businesses.

European Atomic Energy Community Treaty (EURATOM)

Established by the Treaty of Rome 1957, the purpose of EURATOM was to create a specialist market for atomic energy, distribute it through the Community, develop nuclear energy and sell surplus to non-Community states.

EURATOM had its own Commission (which was the equivalent to the ECSC's High Authority) and Council of Ministers, but shared an Assembly and Court of Justice with the European Coal and Steel Community and European Economic Community. EURATOM is another example of sectoral or functional integration.

European Economic Community Treaty (now EC Treaty)

The European Economic Community (now known as the European Community) was established by a separate Treaty of Rome to EURATOM in 1957 and its name was amended to the EC Treaty by the TEU. The aim in the preamble was, 'to lay the foundations of an ever closer union among the peoples of Europe'.

The EEC had its own separate Commission and Council of Ministers but it shared an Assembly and Court of Justice with Euratom and the ECSC.

The Treaty of Rome embodied a very different approach to integration from the ECSC and Euratom Treaties. Whereby the latter attempted to integrate sector by sector, the EEC Treaty concentrates on types of activity rather than particular industries (with the exception of agriculture and transport) and aims to ensure the effective functioning of the market together with free and fair competition. Another characteristic of the Treaty of Rome is that it laid down general principles which are left to the Institutions to work out in detailed measures. Policy making and regulation are left to the Institutions. Timetables were laid down for the elimination of mutual trade barriers and a common external tariff. Through these methods the founders hoped to achieve economic integration which was intended to be the forerunner of political integration. The Treaty was intended as a first step, to be followed by later Treaties which would build on the progress made.

Merger Treaty

The three different communities had created three different sets of institutions, although they shared the same Assembly and Court of Justice. It became inconvenient to have three different sets of institutions so a Merger Treaty came into force in 1967. The three communities themselves did not merge (and have still not merged) but the High Authority and two Commissions merged to form a single Commission and the three Councils merged to form a single Council. Hartley uses the analogy of three commercial companies with the same shareholders and same board of directors. In law, there are three legal persons, in reality there is one.

The most important features of the Merger Treaty have been incorporated into the EC Treaty by the Treaty on European Union.

Single European Act

This was the first major amendment to the EC Treaty. It came about as a result of pressure for increased union and also concern over increased competition from North America and the Far East.

The major amendments were, as follows:

- inauguration of the internal market programme for completion by 31 December 1992;

- introduction of majority voting in Council of Ministers for enactment of certain measures;

- change in implementing powers of Commission;

- creation of co-operation procedure for participation of European Parliament in legislative process;

- recognition of European Council as formal organ of European Community;

- authority granted to Council of Ministers to create the Court of First Instance;

- co-operation in field of foreign policy through European political co-operation;

- co-operation in economic and monetary policy;

- common policy for the environment;

- measures to ensure the economic and social cohesion of the Community;

- harmonisation in the fields of health, safety, consumer protection, academic, professional and vocational qualifications, public procurement, VAT and excise duties and frontier controls.

Treaty on European Union
The most recent amendment to the EC Treaty has been the Maastricht Treaty (officially known as the Treaty on European Union). The TEU creates a European Union, with three pillars – the European Community, Common Foreign and Security Policy and Home Affairs and Justice Policy.

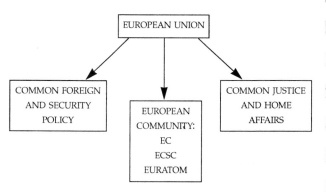

General principles

The Treaty on European Union has provisions on three matters of constitutional importance: human rights, subsidiarity and citizenship.

- Article F(1) enshrines the existing practice that fundamental human rights are to be a general principle of Community law;

- subsidiarity is discussed in more detail in Chapter 2;

- every national of a Member State is a citizen of the European Union;

Economic and monetary union

The Treaty sets out the procedure and timetable for creating Economic and Monetary Union (EMU).

Other changes

The TEU introduces a number of other changes, including:

- establishes a committee of regions;

- Court of Auditors becomes a Community institution;

- greater powers for the European Parliament, with the introduction of a new legislative procedure;

- greater co-operation in the fields of culture, education, vocational training and youth;

- Community will play a role in co-ordinating and liaising between Member States on health care programmes and to raise levels of health protection;

- Community will continue to play a role in consumer protection;

- Community will contribute to the development of trans-European networks;

- Community and Member States will co-ordinate their research and development activities;

- Community shall take action leading to social and economic cohesion;

- Community shall take the environmental aspects laid down in the SEA further by increasing its objectives;

- reaffirmation of the Community's commitment to integrating the economies of the developing nations into the world economy;

- total free movement of capital between Member States and Member States and third countries;

- international rules relating to international transport.

Social Protocol

Eleven of the Member States have agreed to implement the 1989 European Social Charter, the agreement is annexed to a Protocol on Social Policy which is annexed to the EC Treaty.

Opt-outs

The TEU contains a number of opt outs, including:

- UK can opt out from the third stage of EMU;

- UK has opted out of the agreement annexed to the social policy protocol;

The Treaty on European Union has been described as a 'Europe of bits and pieces' by Curtin. This is a reference to the lack of unity contained in the Treaty. The Common Foreign and Security Policy and Justice and Home Affairs pillars of the Union use a different institutional structure to the European Communities pillar, and this contributes to the lack of overall coherence of the Treaty.

Other types of acts between Member States

There are two other types of acts between the Member States subsidiary conventions and acts of the representatives of the Member States.

Subsidiary conventions

Article 220 provides that Member States ought to negotiate conventions to secure for the benefit of their nationals the protection of rights, abolition of double taxation, mutual recognition of companies and reciprocal recognition and enforcement of judgments of municipal courts and arbitration awards. The Treaty on European Union provides for future conventions on justice and home affairs.

Acts of representatives of member States

These occur where members of the Council of Ministers meet not in their capacity as Council members but as ministers of their respective governments. This type of act has been given great prominence by the TEU.

General principles of Community law

In every legal system the written sources of law do not provide the answer to every problem which appears before the courts. The ECJ has therefore to develop general principles of law to provide a foundation for judgment.

Sources of general principles

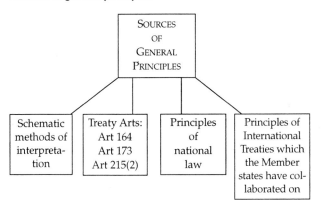

	SOURCES OF GENERAL PRINCIPLES		
Schematic methods of interpretation	Treaty Arts: Art 164 Art 173 Art 215(2)	Principles of national law	Principles of International Treaties which the Member states have collaborated on

The Treaties

The European Court of Justice has declared that a principle laid down in the Treaty is an application of a more general principle not expressly stated in the Treaty. This is then applied in its own right as a general principle of law, eg Art 6 prohibits discrimination on grounds of nationality between Union citizens; this has been promoted into a general principle of equality which forbids discrimination on any ground.

The Treaties also provide more specific justification for the development of general principles of law.

- *Article 164 :* the Court of Justice shall ensure that in the interpretation and application of the Treaty the law is observed. Law in this context must mean something over and above the Treaty itself.

- *Article 173:* this lays down the grounds on which a community act may be annulled. One of these grounds is 'infringement of this Treaty or any rule of law relating to its application'. The phrase 'any rule of law' must refer to something other than the Treaty itself.

- *Article 215(2):* this is concerned with non-contractual liability and provides that the liability of the Community is based on 'the general principles common to the laws of the Member States'.

Principles of the national laws of the Member States
The European Court of Justice has adopted principles of national laws of Member States. It need not be a principle of every Member State. Whatever the origin of the principle, it will be applied by the ECJ as a principle of Community law, not national law.

Principles of human rights in International Treaties
The European Court of Justice in the case of *Nold v Commission* (1974) held that the general principle of fundamental rights was also inspired by Treaties on which the Member States have collaborated on or which they are signatories.

Fundamental human rights
Every Member State is a signatory of the European Convention on Human Rights. The commitment of the Union to human rights was enshrined in Art F of the TEU. This was recognition of a long-standing practice of

acceptance of fundamental human rights as a general principle of Community law starting with the case of *Stauder v City of Ulm* (1969).

The rights which have been recognised by the ECJ include:

- property rights, although these are not absolute and unqualified (*Nold v Commission* (1973));

- religious rights (*Prais v Council* (1976));

- right to privacy (*National Panasonic (UK) Ltd v Commission* (1979)) although it did not extend to seizing goods for purposes of EC competition law;

- right to client lawyer privacy (*AM and S v Commission* (1979));

- due process of law (*Musique Diffusion Francaise SA v Commission* (1983));

- non-retroactivity of criminal law (*Kirk* (1984));

- principle of legal review (*Heylens* (1987)).

Principle of equality
The EC Treaty has specific examples of of equality, as follows:

- suppression of discrimination on grounds of nationality (Art 6) (formerly Art 7);

- discrimination between producers and employers of agricultural products is prohibited (Art 40(3));

- discrimination between employees on grounds of sex is prohibited (Art 119);

The European Court of Justice has taken these specific

examples and deduced from them a general principle of equality (*Frilli* (1972)).

The principle of equality means that persons in similar situations are not to be treated differently, unless the difference in treatment is objectively justified.

Proportionality

This is a principle borrowed from German law. According to this principle a public authority may not impose obligations on a citizen except to the extent to which they are strictly necessary or proportionate to the aim that is being achieved. If a burden is out of proportion then the measure will be annulled. Although the concept is unfamiliar to British lawyers it has been compared to 'reasonableness' and the ECJ has used the term 'reasonableness' on occasion.

Legal certainty

Certainty is a part of most legal systems but in Community law an important concept has developed with various sub-concepts such as non-retroactivity, vested rights and legitimate expectations.

Non-retroactivity and vested rights

The concept of vested rights is often no more than another aspect of retroactivity but it also refers to such matters as the rule of law and the independence of the judiciary. They are rights acquired within the society's legal framework and under due process. The idea is that at any given time a person should know his legal position and rights should not be taken away by retrospective legislation.

There are two rules relating to non-retroactivity. First, legislation is interpreted with a presumption that it is intended not to have retrospective effect. Secondly, although there is a general rule which prevents retroactivity, it is allowed where the purpose of a measure would be defeated provided legitimate expectations are respected.

Legitimate expectations

This is another concept which has been borrowed from German law. It was first applied in *Commission v Council* (1973) 'First staff salaries' case . The Council had agreed a pay formula which was to last for three years for Commission staff. Before the three years had expired the Council attempted to impose a new formula. It was held that the new pay scales were invalid as they infringed legitimate expectations.

The principle will not apply if the applicant is acting outside the ordinary course of business. In *EVGF v Mackprang* (1975) the applicant was buying grain in France and selling it in Germany to take advantage of a devaluation in the French franc. There had been no infringement of legitimate expectations when the Commission authorised German authorities to buy only German grain, as the applicant's actions were purely speculative.

The claimant must also prove not only that he had a legitimate expectation but that there was a causal link between this and his loss (*CNTA v Commission* (1974)).

Legal professional privilege

It was recognised in *AM and S v Commission* (1979) that confidentiality of written communications between lawyer and client was a general principle of Community law but it was subject to two conditions. First, the communication must be for the client's defence. Secondly, the lawyer must be in private practice.

It was held in *National Panasonic (UK) Ltd v Commission* (1979) that there was no violation of a right to privacy if it serves to thwart the enforcement of Community competition law.

Due process and natural justice

This principle has been drawn from English law and requires the making and enforcement of rules of conduct to comply with due process. For example, it was held in *Transocean Paint Association v Commission* (1974) that where a person's interests are affected by a decision of a public authority that person must be given the opportunity to make his view known before the decision is heard.

Equity

The European Court of Justice has also recognised other principles which can conveniently be lumped together under the heading 'equity':

- good faith;

- fairness;

- *force majeure*.

Agreements with third countries

The European Court of Justice applies agreements with third countries as an integral part of Community law. There are three types:

- agreements between the Community and one or more third countries;

- 'mixed' agreements between the Community and Member States on one hand and third countries on the other;

- agreements between Member States and third countries which are only part of Community law in exceptional circumstances.

Legislative acts

The EC Treaty defines three types of legally binding acts:

- regulations;
- directives;
- decisions.

It also includes two non-legally-binding acts:

- recommendations;
- opinions.

Regulations

Article 189 provides that regulations have general application. They are also binding in their entirety and directly applicable in all Member States. For the meaning of 'direct applicability' see Chapter 2. Regulations help ensure uniformity of law throughout the EC. They are normative in character and will apply generally or to groups of people identifiable in the abstract.

Directives

Article 189 provides that directives are binding 'as to the result to be achieved'. They are binding on the Member States and do not bind individuals until they have been transposed into national law. Although they are binding on the Member States the choice of form and methods when transposing them into national law is left to the national authorities. The purpose of directives is to set a common aim for the Member States. The Member States can then use the most appropriate methods for achieving this aim for their own legal system.

It has been held by the ECJ that directives have direct effect as discussed in Chapter 2.

Individuals can apply for compensation when they have suffered loss as a result of the incorrect transposition of a directive, as discussed in Chapter 2.

	Regulations	Directives
Bind	People generally	Member States
Extent to which they bind	In their entirety	Result to be achieved
Need national measures?	No	Must have implementary measures

Decisions

Article 189 provides that decisions are binding on those to whom they are addressed. They can be addressed to individual Member States, corporations or private individuals. They differ from regulations, in that they personally point at people as opposed to applying to people or groups of people in the abstract.

Recommendations and Opinions

Recommendations and opinions have no binding force and are of persuasive authority only. In *Grimaldi v Fonds des Maladies Professionnelles* (1988) the ECJ said that national courts are 'bound to take recommendations into consideration in deciding disputes submitted to them, in particular where they clarify the interpretation of national provisions adopted in order to implement them or where they are designed to supplement binding EEC measures'.

Problems with classification of legal acts

It was held in *Confédération Nationale des Producteurs de Fruits et Légumes v Council* (1962) that the legal classification of a legislative act will depend on its substance rather than its form. An act can be called a regulation but if in substance it is a decision it will be treated as such. Consequently, in *International Fruit Co NV v Commission (No 1)* (1970) what was termed a 'regulation' was, in fact, a bundle of decisions.

Article 189 envisages distinctive roles for each of the different types of legislative acts. In practice, however, there has been a blurring of the different acts. The ECJ has ruled that directives and decisions have direct effect which makes them less distinct from regulations than one would suppose from a casual reading of Art 189. Directives have often been very detailed when their function was to set an aim which would be fulfilled through national implementing legislation. If the directive is highly detailed then the Member State is not left with much discretion to frame the legislation in the most appropriate way to its own legal order.

It has been found that some legislative acts are 'hybrids' and are in part a regulation and in part a decision *per* AG Warner in *NTN Toyo Bearing Co Ltd v Council and Commission* (1977).

The list of acts contained in Art 189 is not exhaustive. The ECJ has held that other types of act are legally binding, for example, in *Les Verts-Parti Ecologiste v European Parliament* (1983) a decision of the Bureau of the European Parliament relating to the distribution of funds prior to the 1984 direct elections was held to be a legally binding act.

2 EC law and national law

Direct effect

Direct effect of treaty provisions

Usually international treaties are agreements between governments and do not create rights for citizens enforceable before national courts.

The Community legal order differs from international law in this respect, as it does create rights for citizens which are enforceable before national courts and this is what is meant by direct effect.

The concept started with the case of *Van Gend en Loos v Nederlandse Belastingenadministratie* (1962). A private firm sought to invoke Community law against Dutch customs authorities in proceedings before a Dutch tribunal. A preliminary reference was made to the ECJ.

The Dutch government argued that an infringement of the Treaty did not give an individual the right to bring an action. Actions could only be brought against the government of a Member State or by the Commission.

It was held that the Treaty created a 'new legal order' which created rights for individuals which became part of their legal heritage.

Van Gend en Loos was brought on the basis of Art 12, which is a negative obligation as it requires that Member States shall refrain form introducing any new customs duties on imports and exports.

The concept was extended in the case of *Lütticke v Commission* (1966) when it was held that a positive obligation could have direct effect once the time limit for implementation has expired.

The criteria for a provision to have direct effect were set out by AG Mayras in *Reyners v Belgium* (1974), as follows:

- the provision must be clear and unambiguous;

- it must be unconditional;

- its operation must not be dependent on further action being taken by the Community or national authorities.

It can be deduced from this that certain provisions of the Treaty are not directly effective as they are too vague. Neither must there be any discretion attached to the implementation of the provision nor must the right be dependent on some legislative or executive action of the Commission of a Member State until such action has been taken or the time limit for taking action has expired.

Van Gend en Loos is an example of what is known as vertical direct effect. The obligation rested on an organ of the state and there was a corresponding right on individuals. It was held in *Defrenne v SABENA (No 2)* (1976) that Treaty obligations could be conferred on individuals as well as Member States, so called horizontal direct effect. The applicant was an air stewardess employed by SABENA. She brought an action against them based on Art 119 which provides that men and women shall receive equal pay for equal work. The applicant claimed that male air stewards were paid more pay for performing exactly the same tasks to stewardesses and this was a breach of Art 119. SABENA argued that the Treaty obligations could be imposed on private persons as well as the State.

Vertical direct effect

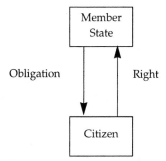

Horizontal direct effect

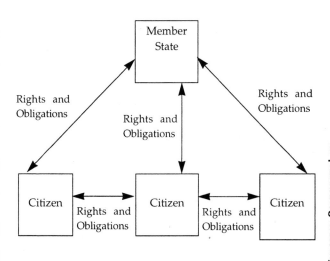

In addition to direct effect there is a principle of 'direct applicability' which means that a provision becomes operative in a Member State immediately without the need for the national legislature to pass implementing legislation to incorporate it into national law.

Certain provisions of the Treaty are directly applicable and there is no need for there to be further legislation by national parliaments incorporating it into national law as it is incorporated already.

The terms direct applicability and direct effect have been used interchangeably by the ECJ, yet they are separate concepts. A provision can be directly applicable in the sense that it forms part of the law of a Member State in the absence of implementing legislation and yet not be sufficiently precise to have direct effect.

Conversely, a Community provision can be sufficiently precise to be relied on before a national court even though it has not been transposed into national law.

Direct effect of regulations

Article 189 states that 'a regulation shall have general application. It shall be binding in its entirety and directly applicable in all Member States'.

As regulations are directly applicable they do not need national implementing legislation. The ECJ has gone further in *Leonesio v Italian Ministry of Agriculture and Forestry* (1971) when it said that not only is national implementing legislation unnecessary, it is illegal.

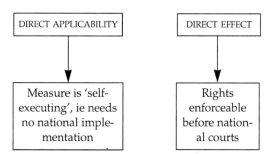

It felt that there would be three main dangers if regulations would be implemented into national law:

- it would be unclear as to whether they took effect from the date of the national measure or the date of the Community measure;

- there would be subtle changes made to the Regulation when it is transferred to national legislation;

- it could prejudice the ECJ's jurisdiction to give a ruling on the interpretation and validity of the measure for the procedure for a preliminary reference.

Nevertheless, there are exceptions to the rule that regulations do not need national implementing legislation:

- where the regulation expressly requires national implementing legislation: *Commission v UK* 'Tachograph case' (1979);

- where a regulation impliedly requires that a Member State brings forward national legislation, eg where the terms of a regulation are vague, though the national legislation must not be incompatible with the regulation;

- a third possible area suggested by Hartley is where a Member State wishes to codify the law in a particular area, ie draw on all the relevant law on one particular topic into one piece of legislation.

To be directly effective and capable of creating rights for individuals enforceable before national courts, they must satisfy the criteria for direct effectiveness:

- the provision must be clear and unambiguous;

- it must be unconditional;

- its operation must not be dependent on further action being taken by Community or national authorities.

Direct effect of directives

Article 189 states that directives are 'binding as to the result to be achieved' but that the choice of 'form and methods' is left to the Member State.

In contrast to regulations the Treaty does not make any reference to them being directly effective, they cannot be directly applicable as they require national implementing legislation to give effect to them.

Despite the Treaty being silent on the point, the ECJ held that directives had direct effect in *Grad v Finanzamt Traunstein* (1970) when a directive specified the commencement date for a provision and a substantive provision of a directive was held to have direct effect in *Van Duyn v Home Office* (1974).

The main reasons why the ECJ gave direct effect to directives was:

- to make them more effective;

- to estop a Member State from relying on its own wrongdoing.

There was a strong reaction against giving direct effect to directives in the Member States, the French *Conseil d'Etat* and the German Federal Tax Court initially denied that directives had direct effect.

The ECJ took this reaction into account, and in addition to having to satisfy the criteria for direct effect, the ECJ has placed two other important limitations on the direct effect of directives:

- they cannot have direct effect before the time limit for implementation has expired: *Pubblico Ministero v Ratti* (1978);

- they do not have horizontal direct effect: *Marshall v Southampton and South West Hampshire AHA (No 1)* (1986).

A directive can be directly effective and may be invoked as such, even though it has been transposed into national law: *Verbond van Nederlandse Ondernemingen v Inspecteur der Invoerrechten en Accijnzen* (1977).

The disadvantages of only giving vertical direct effect to directives have been identified, as follows:

- it restricts the effectiveness of directives within the national legal system;

- it prejudices the uniform application of Community law;

- it discriminates between individuals. For example, in employment law a State employee can rely on a directive as against an employer, whereas a private employee cannot.

As a result of these difficulties the ECJ has had to develop various stratagems to circumvent the problems created by this limitation of on the direct effect of directives. (See below: the interpretive obligation and the creation of effective national remedies). Another of these stratagems has been to widen the definition of the State to enable as many employees as possible to rely on directives.

It was confirmed in the case of *Faccini Dori* (1994) that directives do not have horizontal direct effect but the ECJ suggested that an individual would have other options for enforcing their rights either through indirect effect or under the *Francovich* principle.

Organ of the State

In *Marshall (No 1)* (1984) the UK argued that where the State was acting as an employer it was no different to a private employer. The ECJ rejected this argument and held that it did not matter in what capacity the State was acting, directives could still be relied on against it.

In *Foster v British Gas plc* (1991) it was held that a privatised public utility undertaking was an 'organ of the state' as it was offering a public service under the control of a public authority and therefore had special powers.

While in *Johnston v Chief Constable of the Royal Ulster Constabulary* (1984) it was held that a directive could be relied on against a chief constable as he is responsible for the direction of the police service. Since a police authority is charged by the State with the maintenance of public order and safety, it does not act as a private individual. On that basis it could be regarded as an 'organ of the State'.

Direct effect of decisions

Under Art 189 a decision of the Council or Commission is binding on those to whom it is addressed. It can be addressed either to Member States or to individuals or to corporations.

They were again held in *Grad v Finanzamt Traunstein* (1970) to be directly effective. Again, before they can be directly effective, they must fulfil the criteria for direct effectiveness.

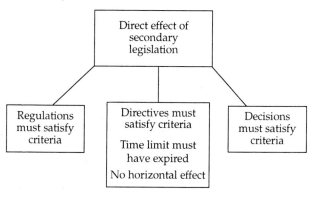

Direct effect of secondary legislation

Regulations must satisfy criteria

Directives must satisfy criteria

Time limit must have expired

No horizontal effect

Decisions must satisfy criteria

Direct effect of international agreements

Agreements with non-Member States have been held to be directly effective, even if they are not directly effective in the non-Member State: *Kupferberg* (1982).

Interpretive obligation (indirect effect)

The main limitations on the direct effect of directives are that they cannot have horizontal direct effect nor can they have direct effect before the time limit for implementation has expired. These limitations meant that the effectiveness of directives has been seriously undermined. The ECJ has created an interpretive obligation on the national courts when interpreting national legislation which to some extent circumvents these restrictions indirectly.

The origins of the obligation are in the case of *Von Colson und Kamman v Land Nordrhein-Westfalen* (1984). A German prison refused to engage two women social workers who were better qualified than the men who were employed in their place. The equal treatment principle had been infringed but the German legislation implementing the directive limited the right to compensation to a limited nominal sum. The directive had not specified the form of the sanction for infringement of the equal treatment principle but it was intended to be an adequate remedy. As there was a discretion in the hands of the Member States as to how the sanction was to be implemented, the provision did not fulfil the criteria for direct effect. On a preliminary reference the ECJ used Art 5 which places Member States under an obligation to fulfil their Treaty obligations.

The ECJ said that Art 5 was an obligation addressed to all national authorities which includes national courts. National courts are therefore under an obligation to interpret national legislation in accordance with the aims and purposes of the Directive.

A limitation was placed on the obligation by the ECJ as it said that it only existed 'so far as it was possible' for the national court to give the national legislation a Community interpretation. Another uncertainty created by the case was that it involved legislation which had been introduced to implement the directive and it was unclear whether the obligation extended to legislation which was not framed with the intention of implementing a directive.

The existence of the obligation was reiterated in *Kolpinghuis Nijmegen BV* (1987) which also added that the obligation existed between the date that the obligation is adopted and the the date of the time limit for its implementation into national law. This raises problems as to legitimate expectations and non-retroactivity. Individuals will have arranged their affairs on the basis of national legislation as it has been implemented and will not have bargained for a re-interpretation which effectively changes the law. In *Kolpinghuis Nijmegen* the ECJ stated that the interpretive obligation was subject to the general principles of legal certainty and non-retroactivity.

The guidelines for the interpretive obligation were recently dramatically extended in the case of *Marleasing SA v La Commercial Internacional de Alimentacion SA* (1992). The plaintiff, Marleasing, sought to set aside the memorandum and articles of association of La Commercial on the grounds that in the view of the plaintiff it had been set up to put certain assets beyond the reach of creditors. The First Company Directive 68/55 exhaustively sets out the grounds on which a company can be declared void and does not list fraud. However, the Spanish had not transposed the directive into their law. Their own Civil Code was enacted before the Directive so could not possibly have been brought forward with the intention of implementing the legislation. Nevertheless, the ECJ in a preliminary reference said that the obligation extended to the Civil Code even though it had been enacted prior to the Directive.

An effect of the ruling was that the plaintiff was able to rely on the Directive against the defendant, even though directives do not have horizontal direct effect, yet this result was achieved by indirect methods. Interestingly, the ECJ specifically said that *Marshall (No 1)* (1984) was good law and that directives do not have horizontal direct effect. Again the ECJ added a qualification to the obligation when it stated that it only existed 'so far as is possible'. A further difficulty was that the ECJ did not state the extent to which the obligation is limited by the general principles of legitimate expectation and non-retroactivity. It had previously stated that these general principles did limit the obligation in relation to criminal cases in *Kolpinghuis Nijmegen* but the situation is unclear in civil cases.

The obligation only exists where there are quite genuinely two possible ways in which to interpret the national legislation, one which accords with the directive and one which does not. In that situation there is an obligation on the national court to give a Community interpretation. This was confirmed in the case of *Wagner Miert v Fondo de Garantia Salariat* (1993).

It is safe to say that the limits placed on the obligation in *Von Colson* and *Marleasing* and the uncertainty surrounding the effect of the general principles of legitimate expectation and non-retroactivity make the scope of the obligation unclear.

The interpretive obligation has the effect of safeguarding the Community rights of those who might otherwise be unable to rely on such rights because of the limitation on the direct effect of directives laid down in *Marshall (No 1)*. However, as Plaza Martin points out, it also has the disadvantage of making the position of defendants uncertain, as they will be unsure as to whether national law needs to be read in the light of the aims and purposes of Community directives or whether it is safe for them to assume that national law has correctly implemented the directive.

Remedies against national governments

In the UK it has been held that infringement by a government department of enforceable Community rights gives rise to a right to judicial review but not to damages: *Bourgoin v MAAF* (1985).

This is now doubtful as a result of the decision in *Francovich and Bonifaci v Italy* (1992). The applicants had been employees in businesses which became insolvent, leaving substantial arrears of salary unpaid. The Italian government had failed to implement a directive which had obliged them to set up a compensation scheme to protect employees of insolvent employers. This breach had been proved in enforcement proceedings which had been taken against Italy.

The provisions of the directive did not have direct effect. Nevertheless, the ECJ held that Art 5 requires Member States to fulfil their Community obligations and that the effectiveness of Community law would be called into question and the the protection of enforceable Community rights would be weakened, if individuals could not obtain compensation when their rights were infringed. On this basis it was said to be inherent from the scheme of the Treaty that individuals should receive compensation from the State when a Member State had breached its Community obligations. This right is subject to three conditions:

- the directive must confer rights on individuals;

- the content of these rights is identifiable by reference to the Directive;

- there is a causal link between the breach of a State's obligation and the damage suffered by the persons affected.

Francovich is obviously a far reaching decision. In the first attempt by a national court to interpret it in *Kirklees Borough Council v Wickes Building Supplies Ltd* (1992) the House of Lords doubted whether *Bourgoin* could be considered good law. Their Lordships said that the liability in damages for breach of a Community obligation rested solely on central government and and local authorities could not be responsible in damages for a breach of obligation.

The decision in *Francovich* will also have a deterrent effect on Member States, since they now face the possibility of paying substantial damages if they are late in implementing a directive, it will concentrate their minds and will encourage them to act on time. It also acts as a penalty on the Member State but this supplements the Member State's liability under Art 171 which was amended by the Treaty on European Union so that Member States which fail to comply with judgments which are the end result of enforcement proceedings can now face penalties under that provision, as well.

A disadvantage of this deterrent effect of *Francovich* has been identified by Martin as a slowing down of the decision-making process with the Member States making sure that directives are drafted with the utmost care prior to adopting them or alternatively they may go to the other extreme and demand that rights are so vague that they could not be relied on by applicants. Another limitation is that the decision attempts to put the applicant in the position he would have been in had the directive been properly implemented, but in some cases money can only be an approximate compensation for what has been lost.

The ambit of the *Francovich* principle has been made clearer by the recent joined cases of *Brasserie du Pêcheur* and *Factortame (No 3)* (1996). Whereas the *Francovich* case made it clear that compensation was payable for non-transposition of a directive, these cases demonstrate that compensation is also available when there has been a negligent transposition of a directive, provided:

- the rule of law infringed must be intended to confer rights on individuals;

- the breach must be sufficiently serious;

- there must be a direct causal link between the State's breach and the injured party's loss.

As to the second condition, the decisive test, is whether there has been a manifest and grave disregard of the limits of the discretion. The factors which a court must take into account are:

- the clarity and the precision of the rule breached;

- the measure of discretion left by that rule to the national or community authorities;

- whether the infringment and damage caused was intentional or involuntary;

- whether any error of law was excusable or inexcusable;

- the fact that a position taken by a Community institution may have contributed to the omission;

- the adoption or retention of national measures or practices contrary to community law.

A breach of Community law will be sufficiently serious if it has persisted despite a judgment that established the infringement, or a preliminary ruling or settled case law of the ECJ has made it clear that the conduct constitutes an infringement.

The national courts must find the facts in the main proceedings and decide how to characterise the breaches of Community law at issue.

Procedural remedies
In addition to the substantive right to damages the ECJ have also ensured the effective protection of Community rights through the creation of effective procedural remedies.

In *Secretary of State, ex p Factortame Ltd (No 1)* (1990) it was held by the ECJ that where a national court considered that the sole obstacle to granting interim relief was a rule of national law then it was obliged to set aside that rule. This ruling has been interpreted as creating a new procedural remedy for the protection of Community rights.

In *Emmott v Minister for Social Welfare* (1990) it was held that where a directive has not been correctly transposed into national law then time does not start to run for the purpose of limitation periods when the directive is properly implemented into national law. This right exists even in respect of non-directly effective rights and also in the absence of the ECJ failing to declare that the Member State has failed to fulfil its obligations. In other words, time does not start to run until an individual is certain what his legal rights are.

However, the *Emmott* principle was not applied in the case of *Steenhorst-Neerings* (1994). The applicant received invalidity benefit. In 1976 it was replaced by a new benefit which excluded married women. This was later reformed but backpayment was limited to 12 months. The ECJ held that the rules were discriminatory but that the *Emmott* principle did not apply to the rule restricting back-payment, as its aim was to ensure good administration and financial equilibrium of the Dutch incapacity system. A further ground for distinguishing between the two cases was that in *Emmott* the rule could not be invoked at all, whereas in *Steenhorst-Neerings* it could be partially invoked.

In *Zuckerfabrik Suderdithmarschen AG v Hauptzollamt Itzehoe* (1991) it was held that the power of a national court to suspend administrative acts which are based on a Community measure whose validity is in doubt can only order a suspension on the same conditions as those applied by the ECJ in interim measure proceedings.

Primacy of EC law

'Twin pillars'

The Community legal order is said to be built on the 'twin pillars' of direct effect and supremacy. The case of *Van Gend en Loos v Nederlandse Administratie der Belastingen* (1963) first stated the principle of supremacy when it held that a Treaty provision took priority over a conflicting piece of earlier Dutch legislation. The case is better known for laying the other pillar of the legal order, namely the principle of direct effect.

The 'twin pillars' of European legal order

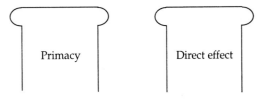

Primacy   Direct effect

The second pillar of the supremacy of Community law was laid in the case of *Costa v ENEL* (1964). The ECJ held that Community law could not be overridden by domestic legal provisions regardless of whether the provisions came earlier or later than Community law.

The basis of the principle of supremacy was found to arise from the words and spirit of the Treaty rather than in national constitutions, which can be seen from a famous piece of the ECJ's *dicta*:

> The transfer by the states from their domestic legal system to the Community legal system of rights and obligations arising under the Treaty carries with it the

permanent limitation of their sovereign rights against which a subsequent unilateral act incompatible with the concept of the Community cannot prevail.

The court argued that a restriction of sovereign rights and the creation of a body of law applicable to individuals as well as Member States, made it necessary for this new legal order to override inconsistent provisions of national law. Community law was also prepared to reach into national law and provide remedies where national did not do so.

Community law overrules provisions of national constitutions

The rule is an unconditional rule and applies to every rule of domestic law, whatever its standing. Consequently, Community law cannot be tested in municipal courts for compliance with constitutions of Member States.

In *Internationale Handelsgesellschaft GmbH v Einfuhr und Vorratsstelle für Getreide und Futtermittel* (1970) it was held that recourse to the legal rules or concepts of national law in order to judge the validity of measures adopted by the Community would have an adverse effect on the uniformity and efficacy of Community law.

Therefore the validity of a Community measure or its effect within a Member State cannot be affected by allegations that it runs counter to either fundamental rights as formulated by the constitution of that state or the principles of a national constitutional structure.

Principle of supremacy must be applied immediately

Primacy is a rule which is addressed to the national courts and is to be applied immediately by every national court.

In *Administrazonie delle Finance dello Stato v Simmenthal SpA*
(1978) an Italian court was faced with a conflict between a
Council regulation and Italian laws, some of which were
subsequent in time to the Italian regulation. Under Italian
law legislation contrary to EC regulations can be declared
unconstitutional but only by the constitutional court and not
by ordinary courts. The Italian judge made a preliminary
reference on the question whether direct applicability of regulations required national courts to disregard inconsistent
subsequent national legislation without waiting for relevant
legislation to be eliminated by national law.

It was held that every national court must apply Community
law in its entirety and must accordingly set aside any provision of national law which may conflict with it.

If national law impairs the effectiveness of Community law
by withholding the power to set aside an inconsistent piece
of national law, then that rule is contrary to Community law.

Member States cannot plead *force majeure*

A Member State cannot say that it has tried to comply with
an obligation or remedy a breach but it has been prevented
by legislature from doing so.

In *Commission v Italy* 'Second Art Treasures' case (1968) an
Italian tax on art treasures was in violation of Italy's obligation under Art 16 to abolish customs duties on exports. The
ECJ held that by continuing to levy the tax they were in
breach of Community law. Legislation had been introduced
but lapsed with the dissolution of the Italian parliament. The
government's inability to to force the legislation through
was not an excuse for failing to give effect to the principle of
supremacy.

This was followed by *Commission v Italy* 'Second Art Treasures' case (1970) when the Commission took enforcement proceedings against Italy for failing to comply with the 1968 judgment as there had been a delay until late 1971 before the tax was abolished and a refund paid to exporters.

The government argued that the legislation had depended upon the legislature which had been unable to bring forward the legislation. The ECJ held that it was a directly applicable provision which did not need national legislation to give effect to it but the court indicated that the principle was wider than this as the Treaties involved a limitation on sovereign rights which could not be overridden by national law.

Similarly, the Court disallowed the claim of a Member State that the payment of a premium for the slaughter of cows under a Community provision was dependent on the adoption of budgetary provisions: *Leonesio v Italian Ministry of Agriculture* 'Slaughtered Cow' case (1972).

Supremacy applies regardless of nature of rule of law
The principle of supremacy applies irrespective of whether the inconsistent provision of national law has a civil or criminal character: *Procureur du Roi v Dassonville* (1974).

A Belgian importer imported Scotch whisky from France in the absence of a certificate of origin from the UK, contrary to the Belgian Criminal Code. As the goods had been acquired from a French agent, obtaining a certificate of origin would have been expensive and difficult.

The Belgian Criminal Court made a preliminary reference asking whether the provisions of the Treaty provided a defence to the proceedings. The ECJ held proceedings contravened Art 30 and no charges could therefore be brought.

Supremacy applies regardless of source of law

In addition to the principle applying regardless of the character of national law it also applies regardless of the source of national law. Both inconsistent statutes and judicial precedents have been declared inapplicable, and rules of professional bodies may also be held inconsistent and applicable: *Royal Pharmaceutical Society of Great Britain* (1989).

Supremacy applies regardless of form of Community law

The principle of supremacy applies to different forms of Community law. Consequently, it will apply whether the Community provision is a Treaty article, a Community act or an agreement with a third country.

Member States must repeal conflicting legislation

Member States are obliged to repeal conflicting national legislation, even though it is not enforced, merely 'inapplicable': *Commission v France* 'French Merchant Seamen' case (1974).

A French law provided that a certain proportion of the crew on French merchant ships had to be of French nationality. This was a conflict with Community law and enforcement proceedings were brought against France. The French government argued that the law had not been applied and as it was regarded as inapplicable, France had not violated the Treaty.

The ECJ held that the existence of the law created 'an ambiguous state of affairs' which would make seamen uncertain as to the possibilities available to them of relying on Community law. It was not enough simply not to enforce the law it had to be repealed.

Interpretation of Community law

Member States cannot give authoritative rulings on the interpretation of Community law.

A classic weapon states use to undermine a Treaty is interpretation. This weapon has been taken away from the Member States as the interpretation of the Treaty has been entrusted to the ECJ under the preliminary reference procedure (see below), but there is a double check because Art 219 provides that 'the Member States undertake not to submit any dispute concerning the interpretation or application of the Treaty to any method of settlement other than those provided in the Treaty'. This puts the ECJ in a monopolist position.

Principle of supremacy and UK law

The British courts faced tremendous difficulties in reconciling the principle of supremacy with British constitutional law. In particular, the courts had to juggle three constitutional conventions of the doctrine of parliamentary sovereignty, the doctrine of implied repeal and the principle that no parliament can bind its successor with the principle of supremacy.

The UK has a dualist constitution and international Treaties will only have the force of law if they have been incorporated into UK law. EC law is incorporated into UK law by virtue of the European Communities Act 1972 which has been amended by the European Communities (Amendment) Act 1986, which incorporated the Single European Act and the European Communities (Amendment) Act 1993 which incorporated the Treaty on European Union. As the UK does not have a written constitution these all have the status of ordinary Acts of Parliament and can therefore be repealed by subsequent parliaments.

The key sections of the 1972 Act are s 2(1) which provides for the direct effect of Community law in the UK. Section 2(2) provides for the implementation of Community law by means of subordinate legislation. Section 2(4), together with s 3(1), in effect provides for the recognition of the principle of supremacy.

The landmark decision with regard to supremacy and UK law is *Secretary of State for Transport, ex p Factortame (No 1)* (1989). The Merchant Shipping Act 1988 was challenged by a group of Spanish fishermen as contrary to Community law. The House of Lords felt that they could not grant interim relief pending the outcome of a preliminary ruling. In its view, an Act of Parliament was presumed to comply with Community law until a decision on compatibility had been given. The Court of Justice held that where a national court is hearing a case which involves questions involving Community law and the national court feels that the sole reason preventing it from granting interim relief is a rule of national law, then it must set aside that rule. Consequently, any Act of Parliament passed after the 1972 Act must be read as subject to directly enforceable Community rights. (See also *Secretary of State for Transport, ex p Factortame (No 2)* (1989)).

In *Secretary of State for Employment, ex p Equal Opportunities Commission* (1994) the House of Lords ruled that rights under the Equal Pay Act and Sex Discrimination Act should be extended to part-time workers despite Parliament's express intention to the contrary.

Subsidiarity

The principle of subsidiarity was introduced into Community law, in matters relating to the environment, by Art 130(4) Single European Act:

> The Community shall take action relating to the environment to the extent to which the objectives referred to in

paragraph 1 can be attained better at Community level than at the level of the individual Member States.

It was made a general principle of Community law by virtue of Art 3(b) Treaty on European Union:

The Community shall act within the limits of the powers conferred upon it by this Treaty and of the objectives assigned to it therein.

In the areas which do not fall within its exclusive competence, the Community shall take action, in accordance with the principle of subsidiarity, only if and in so far as the objectives of the proposed action cannot be sufficiently achieved by the Member States and can therefore, by reason of the scale of the proposed action, be better achieved by the Community.

Any action by the Community shall not go beyond what is necessary to achieve the objectives of this Treaty.

Is subsidiarity justiciable?
Both Toth and Emiliou argue that subsidiarity is not a legal principle at all and that the ECJ is not equipped to decide subsidiarity questions which involve economic and political judgments.

Exclusive jurisdiction and concurrent powers
The subsidiarity principle does not apply to matters which are within the Community's exclusive jurisdiction. At the time of the Treaty on European Union, there seemed to be an assumption on the part of some politicians that concurrent powers were somehow jointly exercised by the Member States and the Community and that subsidiarity would have a role in determining whether these powers would be better exercised by the Member States or the Community.

This is a fundamentally mistaken view as to the nature of concurrent powers. If a power is held concurrently then the Member State can act only up to that the point the Community exercises its rights. Once the Community has acted then it has exclusive jurisdiction and the Member State no longer has jurisdiction to act.

It can be seen from this that the area in which subsidiarity operates is small and only applies to those areas were the Community does not have exclusive jurisdiction or has not exercised its powers where these are held concurrently.

Does subsidiarity contain competing tests?
The principle of subsidiarity has been criticised for containing inherent competing tests. If the action can be more effectively taken by the Member State then it should be taken at that level (the so-called 'test of effectiveness') but if the scale of the action can be better achieved by the Community it should be taken at that level (so-called 'test of scale'). It has been argued that there is an inherent conflict between these two tests. The example has been given of the environment where patrolling of beaches is clearly an activity which can be on its scale better done by local authorities as opposed to the Commission. Nevertheless, it would probably be accomplished more effectively by the Commission which would ensure that standards were uniform across the Community. Which test should therefore be applied the test of scale or the test of effectiveness?

Does subsidiarity already exist in Community law?
There is a view that subsidiarity has existed in Community law since its inception and that the Treaty on European Union has not introduced anything new.

Proportionality is a general principle of Community law which has been inspired by German law. It is a method of protecting fundamental human rights and provides that action must be proportionate to the aim which is being achieved. This acts as a break on the Community's right of action.

Another example of subsidiarity is Art 235. This provides that where the Council lacks the power to achieve a Community objective, it can act by unanimity on a proposal from the Commission to give such power to itself.

It has also been said that directives which leave the choice of form and methods to the Member State is an example of subsidiarity. However, the objective is fixed by the Community itself.

Preliminary references

Article 177 gives the ECJ jurisdiction to grant preliminary references on questions of interpretation and validity of Community law at the request of the national court of a Member State. The procedure is for the national court to hear the case and when it encounters problems relating to interpretation of the Treaties or the interpretation or validity of legislation the case is referred to the ECJ. After a ruling the ECJ returns the case to the national court for it to be applied to the facts, of the case. So, the case starts and ends in the national courts. Article 177 paragraph 2 provides that 'any court or tribunal' has a discretion to request a preliminary reference, but a court against whose decision there is no judicial remedy is obliged to make a preliminary reference under Art 177(3).

Purpose of preliminary references
There are four main purposes to preliminary references:

Uniformity of interpretation
To ensure uniformity of interpretation of Community law

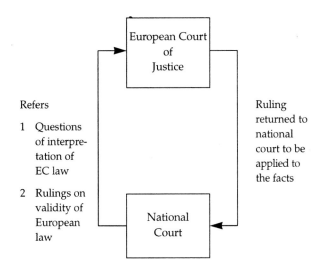

Refers

1 Questions of interpretation of EC law

2 Rulings on validity of European law

Ruling returned to national court to be applied to the facts

throughout the Member States. The principle of supremacy ensures that Community law prevails over national law where the two conflict. This principle would be undermined if the national courts were free to interpret Community law in their own way with the inevitable result that the law would differ from State to State. Preliminary references ensure that there is an authoritative source for interpretation. As there is a written constitution to the European Union, it is possible for secondary legislation to be annulled. Preliminary references ensure that only the ECJ can do this again to avoid discrepancies from State to State.

Familiarise national courts with legal order

They are designed to familiarise national courts with the workings of the European legal order. This has influenced the ECJ's approach to requests for references. In the early days, the ECJ was keen to encourage requests, as without them they would be unable to develop the legal order. Consequently, the ECJ initially were not formalistic in their approach and did not make specifications about the timing or the form of the request. The ECJ also emphasised that the process involved an equal division of labour, it stressed that it was not higher in any hierarchy to the national court but was performing an equal but different role alongside the national courts. This approach was successful and the ECJ currently has a large backlog of requests, which has resulted in a shift of policy. More recently, the ECJ has become much more formalistic, and it has also been argued that it is acting in a more hierarchical manner (see below).

Develop European legal order

The ECJ has used preliminary references to develop the legal order and constitutionalise the Treaties. So it was through requests for preliminary references that the ECJ was able to develop the 'twin pillars' of direct effect (*Van Gend en Loos*) and supremacy (*Costa v ENEL* (1964)).

The ECJ has also been able to extend the scope and effectiveness of the legal order through a combination of preliminary references and Art 5. In this way it has created an interpretive obligation on Member States, to ensure that national courts interpret national legislation in accordance with the aims and purposes of directives: *Von Colson und Kamman, Marleasing*; that individuals receive compensation where they have suffered damage as a result of a Member State breaching its Community obligations: *Francovich* and that there are effective procedural remedies to ensure the protection of Community rights: *Factortame, Emmott, Zuckerfabrik*.

Rulings on direct effect

Preliminary references have also been used to determine whether Treaty provisions and secondary legislation satisfy the criteria for direct effect and can consequently be relied upon by individuals before national courts.

What is a court or tribunal?

Article 177 only permits references from a 'court or tribunal'. Essentially the test for a 'court or tribunal' is a wide one and includes any body with official backing which exercises a judicial function, according to the normal rules of adversarial procedure, and has the power to give binding determinations of legal rights and obligations, independent of the parties in dispute. It is not decisive that the body is recognised as a court under national law (*Corbiau* (1993)).

In *Nederlandse Spoorwegen* (1973) the Dutch *Raad van State* was held to be a court or tribunal within the meaning of Art 177. In theory, an application for judicial review in the Netherlands is decided by the Crown but based on the advice of the *Raad van State*. The ECJ took a pragmatic view and was happy to hold that the *Raad van State* was a court or tribunal within Art 177.

A commercial arbitration tribunal was held not to come within Art 177 in *Nordsee v Reederei Mond* (1982) and this rule applies even if the award of the tribunal can be enforced through the courts.

The situation is different where the arbitration body has some sort of official government backing. Consequently, in *Vassen* (1966) a reference from a body which was an arbitration tribunal but whose members were appointed by the Dutch Minister for Social Security and operated in accordance with ordinary adversarial procedure did come within Art 177.

Similarly, in *Broekmeulen* (1980), a Dutch body called the Appeals Committee for General Medicine heard appeals from a medical disciplinary tribunal. The ability to practice as a medical practitioner was dependent on registration with the committee and one third of the Appeal Committee's members were appointed by the Dutch government. This too was held to be a 'court or tribunal' within the meaning of Art 177.

A tribunal which mixes judicial functions with other functions was still held to be a tribunal within the meaning of Art 177 in *Pretore di Salo v Persons Unknown* (1986).

In *Department of Health and Social Security (Isle of Man) v Barr and Montrose Holdings Ltd* (1991) the Deputy High Bailiff's Court in the Isle of Man was held to come within Art 177 even though only part of the provisions of Community law apply in the Isle of Man, as otherwise the uniformity of Community law would be affected.

The position is unclear as to whether international courts such as the European Court of Human Rights would be able to make a reference.

Lack of jurisdiction
Different problems arose in *Borker* (1980). The applicant was a member of the Paris Bar Council and had been refused permission to appear before a German court. He applied to the Paris Bar Council. It was held that the Paris Bar Council was not a 'court or tribunal' within the meaning of Art 177 as it did not have jurisdiction to decide who appeared before a German court.

When to refer
The question of the national court's timing of a reference can only be understood in the context of the ECJ's changing policy in relation to preliminary references. In the initial stages the ECJ was keen to encourage references as without them it would be unable to familiarise national courts with its

approach and develop the legal order. Emphasis was placed on the co-operative aspects of the procedure and that there was an equal division of labour between the ECJ and the national court. As a result of this policy, the ECJ was relaxed about the timing of references. Similarly, the ECJ has not been formalistic in its approach and in the past if the question has not been properly asked the ECJ reformulates the question and asks itself the question it should have been asked.

In *Henn and Darby* (1979) the ECJ said that it was preferable but not essential for the facts of a case to be decided prior to a reference. The reason for its preference was that it wished to consider as many aspects of the case as possible before giving its ruling.

In the *Creamery Milk Suppliers* case (1980) the Irish High Court requested a ruling without first considering the facts. The ECJ accepted the reference and said that it was entirely for the national court's discretion as to the timing of the reference.

The ECJ became a victim of its success over the working of this co-operative policy. It has developed a backlog of cases and it takes between 18 months to two years for a preliminary reference to be heard by the ECJ. The ECJ no longer feels the need to encourage national courts to make references and in recent cases it has been prepared to take a firmer line on the timing of references.

In both *Pretore di Genova v Banchero* (1993) and *Telemarsicabruzzo SpA v Circostel* (1993) the ECJ held that the national court must define the factual and legal framework in which the questions arise before making a preliminary reference.

In both cases the ECJ said that the questions referred were so vague that they could not be answered. In both cases the ECJ emphasised its role in Art 177 proceedings which is to provide a ruling which which would be useful to a national court in the administration of justice. As both cases involved competition law the facts were particularly complicated which heightened the need for a clear description of the facts. The ECJ is trying to decrease its workload through emphasising its jurisdiction in Art 177 cases.

Discretion to refer

Under Art 177(2) any court or tribunal of a Member State has a discretion to make a reference to the ECJ. This right cannot be curtailed by national law: Second *Rheinmühlen* case (1973) and it cannot be fettered by a regulation of the Communities: *BRT v SABAM* (1973).

Principles under which a British court should exercise its discretion were originally indicated by Lord Denning MR in *Bulmer v Bollinger* (1974):

- The decision must be necessary to enable the English court to give judgment.

- In deciding whether the reference is necessary account must be taken of the following factors:

  ○ the decision of the question must be conclusive of the case;

  ○ is there a previous ruling by the ECJ of the issue?

  ○ is the provision *acte clair*?

  ○ the facts of the case must have been decided.

If the court decides that a decision is necessary it must still consider the following factors:

- delay;

- the difficulty and importance of the point;

- expense;

- burden on the ECJ;

- wishes of the parties;

- difficulty in framing question in sufficiently clear terms to benefit from a ruling.

These criteria have been attacked on the grounds that they are unduly restrictive and delaying because of the expense and burden on the parties may in fact, increase their expenses if a referral has to be made by a higher court.

More recently, the correct approach has been redefined by Sir Thomas Bingham MR in *International Stock Exchange of the United Kingdom and the Republic of Ireland, ex p Else* (1993). In his view three points needed to be considered in deciding whether to make a referral:

- first, find the facts;

- secondly, is the Community law provision critical to the outcome?

- thirdly, can the court resolve the provision of Community law with complete confidence?

In addition, the court must be mindful of four factors when making its decision:

- national law must be fully mindful of the differences between national law and Community law;

- pitfalls of entering into an unfamiliar field;

- need for uniform interpretation;

- advantage enjoyed by ECJ in interpreting Community legislation.

Bingham MR's formulation is weighted more heavily in favour of a referral than Lord Denning's. Walsh feels that there will more successful appeals against the decision to refer under Bingham's formulation than existed previously. He argues that Lord Denning's approach is more subjective and that higher courts are loath to overrule a subjective decision. As Bingham's formulation is much more objective it will be easier for a higher court to overrule a decision to refer.

Obligation to refer

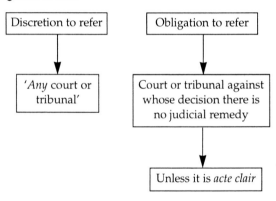

Article 177 paragraph 3 provides that a court or tribunal against whose decision there is no judicial remedy is obliged to make a reference to the ECJ. There are two differing views as to what is meant by the phrase 'a court or tribunal against whose decision there is no judicial remedy'.

- 'Abstract theory': it can only mean the highest court in the land. In the UK it would be the House of Lords only. This view was supported by Lord Denning in *Bulmer v Bollinger*.

- 'Concrete theory': courts which are judging in final instance in that particular case. For example, to appeal from the Court of Appeal to the House of Lords it is necessary to have leave. If leave is not forthcoming then the Court of Appeal is the highest court in that particular case. There is *obiter dicta* supporting this theory in *Costa v ENEL* (1964). In *Hagen* (1980) the Court of Appeal held that it is bound to make a reference under Art 177 if leave to appeal to the House of Lords is not obtainable.

In theory, the Commission can bring enforcement proceedings against a Member State whose highest court does not make a preliminary reference but in practice it does not do so.

Interim proceedings

In *Hoffman-La Roche v Centrafarm* (1978) the question arose whether an interim order given in interlocutory proceedings against which there was no judicial remedy but which could be considered again in the main proceedings was a decision against which there was no judicial remedy? The ECJ emphasised that preliminary references could be made in preliminary references but that there was no obligation to make a reference when the matter could be considered again in the main proceedings.

Acte clair

The ECJ has sanctioned the use of *acte clair* from French law, subject to conditions, where the question is clear and free from doubt. If an act is *acte clair* even a court that comes within Art 177(3) is freed from its obligation to refer.

In *CILFIT v Italian Minister of Health* (1981) the doctrine of *acte clair* was accepted by the ECJ, when it said that an application would not be 'necessary' if:

- the question of Community law was irrelevant;

- the provision had already been interpreted by the ECJ;

- the correct application is so obvious it leaves no room for doubt.

In addition to these criteria the national court must also be convinced that the answer would be equally obvious to a court in another Member State, as well as the ECJ. The national court must compare the different versions of the text in the various Community languages. It must also bear in mind that legal concepts and terminology do not necessarily have the same meaning in Community law as national law.

These last criteria deprive the doctrine of *acte clair* of much of its practical effect. The national judge must be satisfied that not only is the provision free from doubt in his own language but he must peruse the text in the other nine languages and, taking into account the different legal concepts in the different jurisdictions, must be still be satisfied that the matter is free from doubt. An immense challenge even for the most accomplished linguist. The narrowness with which the doctrine has been drawn is a reflection of the advantage the ECJ has over national courts in interpreting legislation and comparing the different texts.

It was held in *Da Costa* that a national court is free to make another preliminary reference, even where the question has been the subject of a previous ruling or where it is *acte clair*.

Validity

In *Foto-Frost v Hauptzollamt Lübeck-Ost* (1985) it was held by the ECJ that national courts could not find Community legislation invalid. So the *acte clair* doctrine cannot apply to questions of invalidity, but it is possible for national courts to find Community acts valid. An exception exists in cases of interlocutory proceedings where national courts for reasons of urgency can rule that Community acts are invalid on an interim basis. In *Zuckerfabrik Süderdithmarschen v Hauptzollmat Itzehoe* (1988 and 1989) it was held a Community act could be declared temporarily invalid, provided:

- it has serious doubts about the validity of the Community act;

- it asks the ECJ for a preliminary ruling on the validity of the act;

- the matter is urgent and the applicant will suffer serious and irreparable damage if relief is refused; and

- due account is taken of the interest of the Community and the need to ensure the effectiveness of Community law.

The ECJ will not overrule a provision of national law in a preliminary reference but it can say that a rule of national law is inapplicable in a Community context by providing guidance on the correct interpretation of Community law.

Can the ECJ refuse to hear a reference?

In recent years this has been one of the most vexed questions in relation to preliminary references and a popular topic with examiners.

The ECJ will decline to hear a reference where it falls outside Art 177. If the reference is not made by a court or tribunal as in *Borker* and *Nordsee* then it will decline to hear a case.

If the reference is nothing to do with Community law then the ECJ will decline the reference: *Alderblum*. The fact that the reference has nothing to do with Community law does not mean that it will have been without merit. The national judge will be free to apply national law safe in the knowledge that Community law is not relevant.

Absence of genuine dispute

In *Foglia v Novello (No 1)* (1979) the questions referred concerned an import tax imposed by the French on the import of wine from Italy. The litigation was between two Italian parties. Foglia was a wine producer and agreed to sell wine to Novello, who was an exporter. In order to challenge the French tax a clause was inserted into the contract that Foglia would not have to pay any duties levied by the French authorities which were in contravention of Community law. The parties were agreed that the tax was illegal and the contractual clause was a device to ensure that the matter could be brought before a court.

The ECJ refused to hear a reference from the Italian court. The ECJ felt that an Italian court was attempting to challenge a French tax and this was abusing the preliminary reference procedure, as it was an indirect method of bringing enforcement proceedings. The ECJ declined to hear the reference on the grounds that there was an absence of a genuine dispute between the parties. The case was returned to the Italian court and the judge re-formulated the questions and referred the matter again to the ECJ. The ECJ again refused to hear the case in *Foglia v Novello (No 2)* (1979).

The case has been criticised on the grounds that the ECJ had entered into a review of the national court's decision to refer. The purpose of Art 177 is that there should be co-operation between national courts and the ECJ. If the ECJ is to enter into inquiries as to whether the national court's decision to refer is a correct decision then it is exercising some sort of appellate jurisdiction. The ECJ had always been keen to emphasise that it performed an equal but different role in relation to Art 177 proceedings but in the *Foglia* cases it suggested, by reviewing decisions of national courts, that it was higher in a hierarchy than national courts.

The approach adopted in the *Foglia* cases has not really been followed in later cases.

Hypothetical questions

In *Mattheus v Doego* (1978) the ECJ refused to hear hypothetical questions relating to the effect that accession to the Community would have on contractual relations of private parties on the basis that the ECJ cannot determine in advance the outcome of negotiations or of the political acts resulting in the admission of a state to the Community.

This was followed in *Meilicke v ADV/ORGA FA Meyer AG* (1991) when again the ECJ refused to hear hypothetical questions. In *Meilicke* a German lawyer had written books and articles in learned journals against the theory of disguised non-cash subscriptions of capital which he submitted was contrary to the Second Company Directive. He held a single share in a company which decided to increase capital by 5 million DM. At an annual general meeting of the company, he tried to find out if the money was used to reduce the company's debts to the bank, which was the guarantor of the newly issued shares. The answers to those questions would determine whether or not the capital amounted to a disguised non-cash subscription. The directors declined to give him the information.

Both *Meilicke* and the company were agreed that contributions in kind would be incompatible with the Directive. There was no real dispute and the proceedings had been contrived so as to ensure that the ECJ answered the questions. The ECJ refused to give a ruling on the basis that they were hypothetical questions and were beyond the jurisdiction of the ECJ as the answers were not needed for the administration of justice. The approach differs from that taken in the *Foglia* cases, as the ECJ is no longer prepared to look at the national court's reasons for making a reference, but instead emphasises the jurisdiction it has been given under Art 177 and the need for national courts to respect its role.

Interpretation and application

There is a division of competence between the ECJ and the national court. The ECJ's role is to give an authoritative ruling as to the interpretation or validity of the Treaty provision or community act, while the national court applies the ruling to the facts of the case. In other words, the ECJ's role is to interpret, while the national court's role is to apply. In *Costa v ENEL* (1964) the ECJ said:

> [Art 177] gives the court no jurisdiction either to apply the Treaty to a specific case or to decide upon the validity of a provision of domestic law in relation to the Treaty, as it would be possible for it to do under Art 169.

The distinction between interpretation and application can be very difficult to make. In addition, an abstract interpretation may not be of assistance to the national court. In the *LTM* case (1966) the national court had informed the ECJ of the facts of the case. When one of the applicants argued that the question was one of application the ECJ replied:

> Although the Court has no jurisdiction to take cognizance of the application of the Treaty to a specific case, it may extract from the elements of the case those questions of interpretation and validity which alone fall within its jurisdiction.

The ECJ varies between a general interpretation and a precise and specific interpretation that only leaves the national court with the task of providing a formal judgment. In *Cristini* (1975), Art 7(2) of Reg 1612/68 provides that a Community national working in another Member State is entitled to the same 'social advantages' as national workers. The French court asked whether a special card to large families enabling them to have reduced rail travel was a 'social advantage'. The ECJ replied that fare reduction cards were a social advantage. Schermers and Waelbrook point out that it is still left to the national court to determine whether the applicant was the widow of a worker within the meaning of the legislation.

Effect of a preliminary reference

A preliminary reference is binding on the national court which referred the question for consideration (*Milch-Fett-und Eierkontor* (1969)).

They may also be cited as precedents in common law jurisdictions (*WH Smith Do-It-All and Payless DIY Ltd v Peterborough City Council* (1990)).

Is a preliminary ruling binding in subsequent cases? If the same issue arises again in a later case the under the doctrine of *acte clair* there is no need to make a further reference. If the national court is unhappy with the previous ruling it can make an additional reference, even if the matter is *acte clair* (*Da Costa*). Indeed, a national court is obliged to follow the ruling or make a new reference. This position is reflected in s 3(1) European Communities Act 1972.

3 Community institutions

The Institutions of the European Community

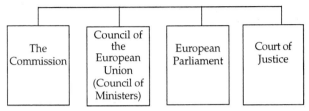

| The Commission | Council of the European Union (Council of Ministers) | European Parliament | Court of Justice |

The Commission

Functions

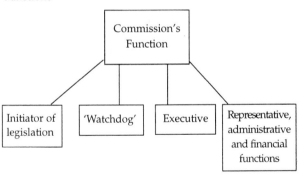

Commission's Function

| Initiator of legislation | 'Watchdog' | Executive | Representative, administrative and financial functions |

Initiator of Community action

The Commission has historically had the right of legislative initiative, and Council decisions are taken on the basis of Commission proposals. The Treaty on European Union allows the European Parliament by an overall majority to 'request' that the Commission submits proposals. Whether 'request' can be interpreted as an ability to demand proposals remains to be seen. Whatever happens, the development is a dilution of the Commission's monopoly over the right of legislative initiative.

It is clear that the Commission shares the right of legislative initiative in respect of the two other pillars of the European Union introduced by the Treaty on European Union. In common foreign and security policy matters the right to submit proposals is shared with Member States. In judicial and home affairs matters, Member States have the right of initiative on all matters, while the Commission has the right of initiative in respect of some matters.

'Watchdog'

The Commission acts as the 'watchdog' of the European Union, either through enforcement proceedings or through its role in competition law.

Arts 169–170. The Commission is in a unique position regarding enforcement proceedings. Under Art 169 proceedings, the Commission can bring Member States which are in breach of their Treaty obligations before the ECJ. The procedure is in two stages. The first is an informal stage whereby the Commission issues a formal notice and eventually issues a reasoned opinion to the Member State which delimits the nature of the dispute. In practice, the Commission attempts to negotiate a settlement with the Member State and in 1990 approximately 78% of cases were settled at the informal stage. The second stage is the formal litigation stage where the Commission brings the errant Member State before the ECJ.

Article 170 proceedings involve one Member State taking another Member State before the ECJ, but even with this procedure the Member State must first take its complaint before the Commission, which will issue a reasoned opinion. In practice, if there is substance to the complaint then the Commission will take the complaint over, and consequently Art 170 is rarely used.

As the Commission is involved in all enforcement proceedings and negotiates the outcome of most such proceedings it is in a distinctive position. Snyder 56 MLR 19 argues that this enables the Commission to use litigation to develop long-term strategies and establish basic principles. For example, in the years prior to 1 January 1993 deadline for the European Internal Market, most enforcement proceedings related to the non-implementation of directives. Article 169 was being used as a tool to ensure the success of the Internal Market programme.

Competition law. The Commission is also the watchdog for the Community's competition law policy. Under Regulation 17/62 it has the power to impose fines and penalties on individuals for breach of Arts 85 and 86.

It also is the only body empowered to grant exemptions for restrictive agreements under Art 85. These can take one of two forms: an individual or block exemption. As the Commission is the only body empowered to grant exemption, its unique position enables it to formulate its own policies in respect of them. Whish argues that block exemptions become in fact a 'model' agreement and therefore imposes conditions on the parties which they would not agree to if they had been allowed freely to negotiate contracts. Also, it can be seen that the nature of individual exemptions has changed, in response to changing economic circumstances. Initially, it favoured granting exemption to agreements made between small and medium-sized enterprises. More recently, in response to an increasing threat from American and Japanese competition, it has been more prepared to grant exemption to large enterprises to enable them to better compete on a global scale.

Executive of the Community

The Commission is often called the executive of the Community. The term is misleading and the Commission's role has fluctuated between a prototype federal government and a secretariat simply carrying out the instructions of the Council of Ministers. The change in role has been a response to historical circumstances. Unlike the Parliament which has seen a steady increase in its powers since the Treaty of Rome; the Commission has seen peaks and troughs in its powers. The key dates are as follows:

1958–1965. This period was the highpoint of the Commission's powers, when it seemed to be evolving into some sort of federal government. It negotiated the elimination of customs tariffs and a common agricultural policy, although it had less success with the establishment of a common external tariff, internal liberalising measures and energy and transport policy.

1966. Luxembourg compromise. In response to a constitutional crisis in the Community this convention was developed. Where the vital interests of a Member State are at stake then it can veto a legislative proposal. The Community was put on a more intergovernmentalist footing and the Commission took on more of the characteristics of a secretariat.

1974. Formation of the European Council. This again gave a more intergovernmentalist flavour to the Community.

1986. Single European Act. The 1993 deadline enhanced the Commission's role. It became more active in the legislative sphere and in negotiation with national governments.

1993. Treaty on European Union. The Commission was on the wane again. Right of legislative initiative diluted. The new legislative procedure in Art 189b only allows for the Commission to mediate in the Conciliation Committee and its proposals can be amended by a qualified majority. This weakens the Commission as it makes its proposals easier to change.

Commission's powers

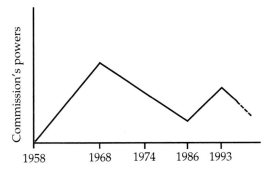

The Commission has a small primary legislative power. In *France, Italy and UK v Commission* (1980) it was held that the Commission had a right to legislate where it is clear from a purposive interpretation of a Treaty provision that it was intended to give such a right to the Commission.

The Commission is often involved in the detailed implementation of Council decisions. This frequently involves further legislation and the Commission has been given wide powers of delegated legislation. The Council has not relinquished total control over the delegated legislation and retains varying degrees of control through the committee's system.

Recommendations and opinions
The Commission can formulate recommendations or opinions on matters dealt with in the Treaty.

Representative, financial and administrative functions
The Commission has a number of representative, financial and administrative functions.

It represents the Member States in negotiations with non-Member States.

It is responsible for the administration of Community funds.

Composition
There are 20 members of the Commission, who are appointed by the governments of the Member States. They must all be nationals of the Member States and no more than two may be nationals of the same State. In practice, each of the five larger States – France, Italy, Germany, Spain and the UK – have two Commissioners and the smaller States have one each.

Under Art 11 Merger Treaty the Commissioners must be appointed by 'common accord'. Each appointment must be agreed to by all the Member States and as a result of the Treaty on European Union, the Parliament can veto the appointment of Commissioners.

Despite the careful attention to the representation of each Member State, Commissioners are not the representatives of national governments and are required to act in the interests of the Union, as a whole. They are required to be above national loyalties.

The Commission acts as a college and it must be agreed on a proposal before it is sent to the Council. It is headed by a President and there can be one or two Vice-Presidents.

There are 23 departments known as Directorates General. Each Directorate General is headed by a Director General, who is responsible to the relevant Commissioner. Directorates General are sub-divided into Directorates (headed by a Director) and these in turn are made up of Divisions (each under a Head of Division).

Each Commissioner is assisted by his Cabinet, which is a type of private office and consists of a group of officials appointed by him and directly responsible to him. The head of the Cabinet is known as the Chef de Cabinet. The Chefs de Cabinet meet regularly to co-ordinate activities and prepare the ground for Commission meetings. If the Chefs de Cabinet reach unanimous agreement on a question then their decision is normally adopted by the Commission without debate.

Commissioners are appointed for five-year renewable terms. All the terms expire together, so the whole of the Commission is re-appointed at the same time. National governments cannot dismiss the Commission during a term of office; they can only fail to renew a term.

The Commission can be forced to resign *en bloc* by the Parliament, but this cannot be used to dismiss individual Commissioners.

The ECJ can compel a Commissioner to retire on grounds of serious misconduct or because he no longer fulfils the conditions required for the performance of his duties.

Council of the European Union (formerly the Council of Ministers)

The purpose of the Council of the European Union is to represent the peoples of the Member States.

Functions

Its functions are:

- take general policy decisions;

- ensure objectives set out in Treaty are attained (Art 145);

- ensure co-ordination of general economic policies of Member States (Art 145);

- power to take decisions (generally based on Commission proposals);

- conclude agreements with foreign countries;

- jointly decide budget with Parliament.

Composition

The Council is not a fixed body, each Member State is represented by a government minister. The government minister who attends the meeting will depend on the subject matter of the meeting. When general matters are discussed, the Member States are represented by their foreign ministers and it will be called a 'general council'. In addition, there are 'specialised' or 'technical' councils where the Member States will be represented by the government minister responsible for that particular specialisation.

Presidency

The Presidency of the Council rotates amongst the members at six-monthly intervals. While it holds the Presidency, a Member State will provide a President (chairman) for all meetings of the Council. The President will call meetings, preside at them, call for a vote and sign acts adopted at the meeting. The Presidency also has responsibility to ensure the smooth running of the Council, will act as mediator between the Member States when searching for an agreement and is the Union's representative to the outside world.

To a large extent the Presidency will enable a Member State to control the agenda of the European Union, so a Member State will attempt to use the time that it holds the Presidency to push through as many measures as possible.

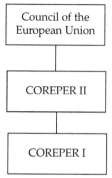

```
┌─────────────────────┐
│   Council of the    │
│   European Union    │
└─────────────────────┘
           │
           │
┌─────────────────────┐
│     COREPER II      │
└─────────────────────┘
           │
           │
┌─────────────────────┐
│     COREPER I       │
└─────────────────────┘
```

COREPER

The government ministers who comprise the Council of the European Union will have full-time ministerial responsibilities in their own country and as a result are only present in Brussels for short periods.

In order to provide continuity, a Committee of Permanent Representatives, known as COREPER was established.

Each Member State has an ambassador to the Union and these ambassadors are given the title permanent representatives. Their function is to represent the Member States at a lower level than the Ministers.

In fact, there are two tiers to COREPER itself. Important political questions are dealt with by the permanent representatives themselves, this is known as COREPER II.

More technical questions will be dealt with by deputy permanent representatives meeting known as COREPER I.

At a lower level still COREPER is involved in the work of a plethora of subcommittees and working groups which examine Commission proposals. In these meetings the Member State is often represented by a national expert.

COREPER has been called a 'mixed' institution, part of a 'grey zone' of institutions which cannot be classified as belonging either to the Union or to Member States.

Hayes-Renshaw, Lequesne and Mayor Lopez 28 JCMS 119 discovered that while the permanent representatives carry out the instructions of their national capitals, they also develop a loyalty to each other as a group built up over a course of dealing consisting of many hours of meetings. Their desire to defend national interests is matched by a desire to reach agreement, they perceive a necessity to engage in 'log-rolling': trading compromises on one issue in return for concessions on another unrelated matter, in order to reach agreement.

They also saw their role as educating their national governments as to the nature of the decision-making process, and acting as a bridge between experts from the Commission and Member States on one hand and Commissioners and national governments on the other.

Voting

Article 148(1) provides: 'Save as otherwise provided in this Treaty, the Council shall act by a majority of its members'.

In practice, only a few unimportant matters are decided by a simple majority. Some matters, eg admission of new members, are decided unanimously. Most matters are decided by a 'qualified majority', where the votes of larger States have greater weight than the votes of smaller ones. Under Art 148(2) the votes of the Member States are weighted as follows:

Germany, France, Italy, UK	10 votes (each)
Spain	8 votes
Belgium, Greece, Netherlands, Portugal	5 votes (each)
Sweden, Austria	4 votes (each)
Denmark, Ireland, Finland	3 votes (each)
Luxembourg	2 votes

Total: 87

A qualified majority is 62 votes.

Luxembourg Accords
In addition to the above rules, there is a constitutional convention known as the 'Luxembourg Accords', which requires that discussions be continued until unanimity is achieved before a decision can be taken which affects the vital national interests of a Member State.

This does not have the force of law but has been followed in practice. The veto will not be allowed where its use is 'improper'. In May 1982 the UK attempted to invoke the veto to prevent an increase in the price of agricultural products. It was conceded by the UK that the issue did not involve vital national interests but they were attempting to force concessions on another issue. This was not accepted by the other Member States as a proper use of the veto and the proposals were adopted. This incident was a watershed and marked the beginning of the decline the Luxembourg Accords. It was no longer left to the Member State to define what its vital national interests were.

The Single European Act seems to have put an end to the Luxembourg Accords. Despite the British Foreign Secretary telling the House of Commons in 1986 and 1990 that they were unaffected by the Single European Act, the only attempt to use the veto since the Act came into force (by Greece in 1988) was unsuccessful. This led Teasdale in (1993) 31 JCMS 567 to declare that '... the Luxembourg Compromise effectively died with the Single European Act'.

Tactics have essentially changed in relation to legislation which is not liked by Member States. The UK's current tactic is to challenge the legal basis of disputed legislation rather than seek to impose a veto.

European Council

In 1974 it was agreed that the heads of government of the Member States, together with their foreign ministers, would hold summit conferences at regular intervals. These became known as the 'European Council' and achieved legal status by virtue of Art 2 Single European Act. The President of the Commission has also been given the right to attend meetings.

The title 'European Council' is confusing, since it is different to the Council of the European Union, although it can act as a Council of the European Union, as there is nothing to prevent Member States being represented by their heads of government.

The European Council possesses no formal powers. It is a forum for discussions, on an informal basis, relating to issues of common Community concern and it is a vehicle for co-ordinating the Member States' foreign policies to ensure that they maximise their influence on world affairs. To this end the Single European Act places an obligation, 'to endeavour jointly to formulate and implement a European foreign policy'.

Article D of the Treaty on European Union provides a further role for the European Council when it states that it shall '... provide the Union with the necessary impetus for its development and shall define the general political guidelines thereof'. The European Council is the focus of the inter-governmentalist activities under the Common Foreign and Security and Justice and Home Affairs pillars of the European Union.

The Presidency of the European Council is held by the Member State holding the Presidency of the Council of Ministers.

European Parliament

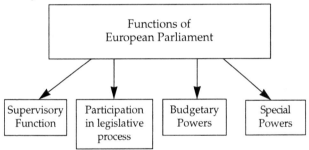

Purpose: to represent the peoples of the Member States.

Seats:

Germany	99
France, UK, Italy	87 (each)
Spain	64
Netherlands	31
Belgium, Greece, Portugal	25 (each)
Sweden	22
Austria	21
Denmark, Finland	16 (each)
Ireland	15
Luxembourg	6
Total:	610

Powers and duties

The powers of the European Parliament can be categorised as follows:

- supervisory function;
- participation in legislative process;
- budgetary;
- special powers.

Supervisory function

The Commission is politically accountable to the Parliament. The Parliament consequently has a number of powers to hold the Commission accountable:

- the Commission has to reply orally or in writing to questions put to it by the Parliament (Art 140);
- can demand resignation of Commission *en bloc*;
- debates the annual report produced by the Commission;
- system of Parliamentary Committees which prepare decisions of the Parliament and maintains regular contact with the Commission when the Parliament is not sitting;
- members of the Commission participate in Parliamentary debates;
- Parliament uses its budgetary powers to hold the Commission accountable.

It has been argued that the supervisory powers over the Commission are too powerful to be used. Although it can demand the resignation of the Commission *en bloc*, the old Commission would continue until a new Commission is appointed by the governments of the Member States and the Parliament had no say in the appointment of a new

Commission. The Treaty on European Union rectifies this by giving the Parliament a power of veto over the appointment of Commissioners, so the Parliament's hand has been strengthened in relation to this power. The problem is that the Parliament does not usually have an argument with the Commission as the two institutions are natural allies, both seeing things from a Community perspective while the Council which represents the interests of the Member States has a more nationalistic approach.

The Parliament also exercises supervisory powers over the Council. Although not obliged to do so, the Council replies to written questions and through the President of the relevant Council formation, to oral questions. Council Presidents are invited to appear before Parliamentary committees and attend plenary sessions to give the views of Council or give an account of Council business. A problem in supervising the Council arises from the fact that it represents the national interest and therefore speaks with a discordant voice.

The Treaty on European Union has given additional supervisory powers to the Parliament:

- Parliament will have the right to set up temporary Committees of Inquiry to investigate 'alleged contraventions or maladministration in the implementation of Community law' (except where the matter is *sub judice*);

- any citizen of the Union or any resident of a Member State has the right to petition the European Parliament on a matter within Community competence which affects him directly;

- the Parliament is to appoint an Ombudsman who will be empowered to receive complaints concerning instances of maladministration in the activities of Community institutions or bodies (except the Court of Justice and Court of First Instance).

Participation in the legislative process

There are four components of the legislative process: consultation procedure, co-operation procedure, co-decision procedure and assent. The relevant procedure and consequently the Parliament's involvement in the process is governed by the Treaties.

Procedure without consultation. The most significant area in which legislation can be adopted without any involvement of the European Parliament is that of the common commercial policy. All that Art 113 requires is a Commission proposal and adoption by the Council, acting by a qualified majority. In practice, the Commission usually suggests that the Parliament be consulted on an optional basis and the Council frequently follows this advice. As there is no guaranteed place for the Parliament in the procedure referred to in Art 113, a strict interpretation of the notion of commercial policy is called for.

Consultative function. One of the Parliament's main functions has traditionally been to advise and be consulted on proposed legislation. Prior to the Single European Act, the Treaties only gave the European Parliament a right to be consulted in the legislative process. The tendency is to limit the use of the consultation procedure to economic sectors of special political sensitivity in the Member States, or matters felt to impinge directly on sovereignty. The consultation procedure still exists in relation to the Common Agricultural Policy, decisions on own resources, decisions under Art 235, provisions relating to aspects of environmental policy, harmonisation of indirect taxation, decisions on how a European Union citizen can exercise his right to vote and stand in municipal and European elections, visa policy and several articles relating to Economic and Monetary Union.

The Commission forwards a proposal to the Council, which in turn forwards it to the Parliament for its opinion. The proposal is passed to the appropriate Parliamentary Committee before a plenary session of Parliament gives its opinion. There is no obligation on the Commission or the Council to follow this opinion. However, failure to consult the Parliament where there is a Treaty requirement to do so is a breach of an 'essential procedural requirement' and the legislation will be annulled (*Roquette Frères v Council* (1979) and *Maizena v Council* (1980)).

The Parliament must be reconsulted if the Commission amends the proposal or the Council intends to use its own power of amendment, and the resulting text, considered as a whole, differs in substance from the one which was the subject of the original request for an opinion (Case C-65/90 *European Parliament v Council* (1992)).

There is no requirement on the Commission to consult the Parliament while formulating a proposal. However, the Parliament can use its supervisory power over the Commission to indirectly influence the Council in the consultation procedure. The Council takes its decisions on the basis of Commission proposals. The Commission would want its proposals to enjoy broad support from the Parliament as the former is accountable to the latter. In this indirect way the Parliament can bring pressure to bear to ensure that its opinions are respected. The Parliament's power over Commission proposals has been strengthened by the Treaty on European Union, which provides that the Parliament can 'request' proposals from the Commission. It remains to be seen whether 'request' will be interpreted as meaning that the Parliament can demand Commission proposals and share the right of legislative initiative.

Certain provisions of the Treaty require the Council, before taking a decision, to consult, either in addition or instead of the European Parliament, other Community institutions or bodies. Previously the only body to be consulted was the Economic and Social Committee and the Court of Auditors in relation to financial legislation. The TEU extends the range of bodies from which opinions must be sought. In particular it provides for a Committee of Regions.

In the context of Economic and Monetary Union, the TEU has introduced variants of the consultation procedure, tailored to accommodate the role of the European Central Bank (ECB) in the management of monetary policy and the Bank's relationship with the Community institutions. For example, the system of rules laid down in the Statute of the European System of Central Banks (ECSB) is expressed in the alternative: the Council may either act on a proposal from the Commission and after consulting the European Parliament and the ECB or on a recommendation from the ECB and after consulting the European Parliament and the Commission. On some decisions the Parliament only has the right to be informed, while the decision irrevocably fixing exchange rates is to be taken on a proposal by the Commission, after consulting the ECB alone.

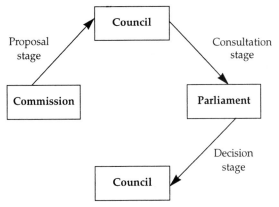

Co-operation procedure (Article 189c). The Single European Act introduced a new legislative procedure which gave the Parliament greater say over legislation. This involves two readings on the part of the Council and the Parliament. Initially the co-operation procedure was used for legislative measures for completion of the Internal Market, in the following areas:

- discrimination no grounds of nationality;

- free movement of persons;

- freedom to provide services;

- harmonisation of laws under Arts 100A and B;

- improvement of health and safety of workers;

- implementation of decisions relating to the European Regional Development Fund;

- adoption of research and technological development programmes.

The Treaty on European Union has brought a significant change to the co-operation procedure and for most of the decisions for which the co-operation procedure was required the co-decision procedure will now be used. New uses have been created for the co-operation procedure and it is now used in connection with the common transport policy, vocational training, environment and common development co-operation. Its use has been retained for decisions implementing the European Regional Development Fund.

The co-operation procedure works by following initially the same procedure as the the consultation procedure but the Council will adopt a 'common position' at the end of this first reading.

The Parliament can approve the 'common position' or do nothing for three months, in which case the 'common position' will be adopted.

The second option is for the Parliament to reject the 'common position' by an absolute majority of its members. The Council can still adopt the legislation, but only if it acts unanimously.

The third option is for the Parliament to propose amendments to the 'common position' by an absolute majority of its members. The Commission must then re-examine the proposal and either adopts the Parliament's proposals or leaves its own original proposal intact. The re-examined proposal is sent back to the Council which can adopt it by a qualified majority or amend it unanimously.

Although the co-operation procedure does not give a power of veto to the Parliament, it forces the Council to take account of its views more directly than the consultation procedure.

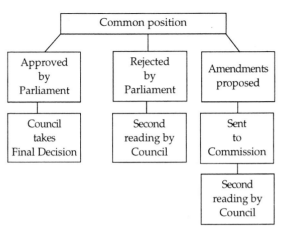

Co-decision procedure (Art 189b). Technically, it is incorrect to call this procedure 'co-decision', as it does not give the Parliament equal rights of approval over the legislative procedure. Nevertheless, the Parliament's influence over legislation has been increased still further where the procedure has been used. The correct term is the 'procedure referred to in Art 189b'.

The procedure is for the Commission to send its proposals to both the Council and the Parliament. Apart from this the procedure for first reading is the same as for the co-operation procedure.

The question arises whether the case law of the ECJ on the reconsultation of the ECJ, should the Council be disposed to adopt a common position differing in substance from the original proposal applies in the present case where, strictly speaking, there was no consultation of the Parliament by the Council in the first place, each institution having received the proposal separately from the Commission independently.

Dashwood argues that there should be reconsultation, as the Council should be apprised of the Parliament's view on the position it is proposing to take, before that position suffers the crystallisation which is bound to result from the incorporation of a provisional legal act. He rejects the idea that the Parliament has ample opportunity to voice its disapproval at second reading.

This would place the Parliament at a disadvantage as it can act by a simple majority at First Reading, whereas it must propose amendments by an absolute majority of its members on Second Reading.

The Second Reading is set in motion by communication of the common position to the Parliament, with a full explanation of the Council's motive. The Council will adopt a common position which can be approved, rejected or amended by the Parliament.

If the Parliament approves or fails to signify its intentions then the measure is adopted.

If the Parliament rejects the 'common position' then the Council may convene the Conciliation Committee which consists of equal members of the Council and Commission with the Commission acting as an honest broker. If the Parliament still rejects the 'common position' then the measure is effectively vetoed and will lapse.

Where the Parliament proposes amendments, the amended text is sent to both the Council and the Commission. The Council can within three months (which can be extended by common accord by one month) accept and adopt this amended proposal (acting by a qualified majority except in respect of amendments on which the Commission has delivered a negative opinion, where the Council must act unanimously) or if it is not accepted then the Conciliation Committee can be convened to agree a joint text.

If no joint text is approved, the measure either lapses or the Council can adopt it on a unilateral basis unless an absolute majority of the Parliament moves to reject the text. A free hand is given to the Conciliation Committee in negotiating the joint text which need bear no relation to the common position adopted by the Council, nor does it need the approval of the Commission. Dashwood submits that in order to avoid infringement of the Commission's power of initiative, the joint text must, at least, relate to the same subject matter as the original proposal.

Decisions of the Conciliation Committee are an exception to the general rule that the Council can only amend Commission proposals unanimously. In other words, at the conciliation stage the European Parliament and the Council escape from the logic of the second reading which aims at a solution based on the common position.

Where the Conciliation Committee does not approve a joint text, the proposed act shall be deemed not to be adopted unless the Council, acting by a qualified majority within six weeks of expiry of the period granted to the Conciliation Committee, confirms the common position to which it agreed before the Conciliation Committee was initiated. The act will be finally adopted unless the European Parliament, within six weeks from the Council's confirmation, rejects the text by an absolute majority of its component members, in which case the proposed act is not adopted. At this third reading the Council can override the Parliament's objections, although Parliament has another chance to reject the text.

The Council's power is limited to that of confirmation of the common position agreed before the conciliation committee was initiated, possibly with amendments proposed by the European Parliament. Paragraph 6 talks of the Council acting by a qualified majority and does not say expressly that it must act unanimously if an amendment was the subject of a negative Commission opinion. Can the Council confirm such amendments on a third reading by a qualified majority or does the general rule in Art 189a(1) apply? The point is ambiguous and can only be resolved by the ECJ.

The Art 189b procedure is used for internal market legislation which used to be subject to the co-operation procedure (see above). In addition it applies to the following areas:

- consumer protection;

- trans-European networks;

- some environmental measures;

- incentive measures in the field of culture;

- adoption of multinational framework programme for research.

The procedure in Art 189b has brought about a major transformation in the role of the Parliament in law making. The consultation and co-operation procedures enable the Parliament to put political pressure on the Commission to take up some or all of its amendments.

Under Art 189b the Parliament can directly influence the outcome, through negotiation in then Conciliation Committee or through its use of veto.

The Council acting on its own or in alliance with the Commission can no longer override the wishes of the Parliament.

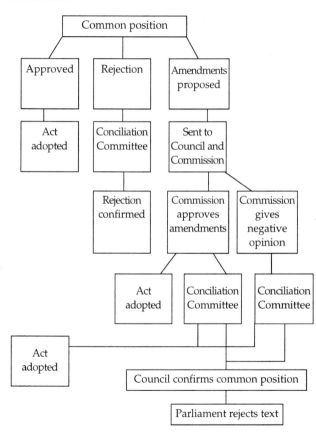

Assent procedure. The assent procedure was introduced by the Single European Act and can properly be called co-decision, as it requires the approval of Parliament before the Council can adopt an act. Originally, the Parliament's approval was required for the admission of new members and for the conclusion of association agreements.

The category of agreements to which it applies has been considerably enlarged by the Treaty on European Union. It now applies to more international agreements and in certain cases the legislative sphere:

- legislation concerning the exercise of free movement and residence rights;

- acts defining the tasks, policy objectives and organisation of structural funds;

- decision to set up Cohesion Fund;

- amendment of certain provisions of the Statute of European System of Central Banks (ESCB);

- acts regulating elections to the European Parliament.

Lack of transparency. The variants on the number of decision-making procedures has been criticised for creating a lack of transparency.

Budgetary powers

The Parliament's powers in relation to the budget were significantly increased by the Budgetary Treaties of 1970 and 1975. As a result of the latter Treaty the Parliament now jointly exercises control over the budget with the Council, although since 1988 it does so within the context of 'budgetary discipline'.

The Council has the final say over 'compulsory expenditure', which consists mainly of expenditure on the Common Agricultural Policy, and the Parliament has the final say over 'non-compulsory expenditure' which relates mainly to social and regional policy, research and aid to non-European Union countries such as Russia and countries in Eastern and Central Europe.

The powers are less impressive than they first appear. The majority of expenditure is compulsory but the proportion of non-compulsory expenditure has been increasing in recent years. There are also restrictions on the amount that non-compulsory expenditure can increase.

A disagreement between the Council and Parliament as to the increase of non-compulsory expenditure lead to the ECJ annulling the adoption of the budget by the President of the Parliament in *Council v European Parliament* (1986).

Since then, inter-institutional agreements have led to the Commission, Council and Parliament agreeing 'financial perspectives', fixing annual ceilings for various categories of expenditure.

The Parliament can also reject the draft budget in its entirety and has done so on three occasions.

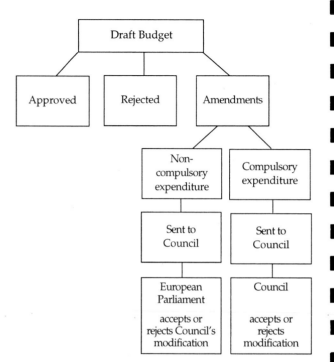

Special powers

The Parliament has a number of powers not directly connected with its supervisory, legislative or budgetary functions.

It has the right to approve amendments of the Treaty in the case of 'small' revisions of the ECSC Treaty.

It has power over its own internal organisation, such as laying down rules of procedure. It also has the power to adopt appropriate measures to ensure the due functioning and conduct of proceedings. In *Luxembourg v European Parliament* Case 230/81 the Luxembourg government failed in its attempt to stop the Parliament dividing its plenary sessions between Luxembourg and Strasbourg. Limits were found to exist in relation to this power in *Luxembourg v European Parliament* Case 238/81 when it was held that the Parliament could only move staff to Strasbourg and Brussels to the minimum extent necessary to ensure the efficient working of the Parliament.

Parliament and the European Court of Justice

Historically, the Parliament has been weak and it has constantly been attempting to extend its role and increase its power and influence. One method that the Parliament has developed of putting pressure on the Council to take decisions has been to take it to the ECJ.

Failure to act. In *European Parliament v Council* (1985) Case 13/83, the ECJ held that the Parliament could bring proceedings against the Council under Art 175 for failure to act when the Council had been in breach of its Treaty obligations because it had failed to adopt a common transport policy. Although the Court held that the Council should have acted, it was not prepared to say what the content of the Council's provisions should have been.

Action to annul. Although the right to bring an action for failure to act was granted readily, there was initially far more reluctance on the part of the ECJ to allow the Parliament privileged status in bringing actions for the other type of judicial review, 'actions to annul' under Art 173. A long line of cases, eg *European Parliament v Council* (1988) Case 377/87 and *European Parliament v Council* (1988) Case 302/87, held that the European Parliament did not have power to bring annulment proceedings. Eventually it was held in *European*

Parliament v Council (1990) Case 70/88 'Chernobyl' case that the Parliament could bring an action to annul where there had been an infringement of the Parliament's rights and the action was taken in order to safeguard those rights.

Actions against Parliament. The Parliament can also be a defendant as well as a plaintiff before the Court of Justice. The original intention of the Treaty framers was that the Parliament should be liable for its decisions in staff cases. Liability has since been extended and the ECJ has held that the Parliament can be a source of 'justiciable acts' and can be sued under Art 173 (actions to annul), despite the fact that Art 173 does not refer to the Parliament. This has lead to other Community Institutions and individuals (other than staff) challenging the decisions of the European Parliament.

So in *Les Verts – Parti Ecologiste v European Parliament* (1983) a French political party was able to obtain annulment of European Parliament Bureau decisions concerning the distribution of funds to political parties who participated in the 1984 Euro elections.

Similarly, in *Council v European Parliament* (1986) Case 34/86, the Council obtained a ruling that the decision of the President of the Parliament declaring the 1986 budget adopted was illegal.

This does not mean that all acts of the Parliament are 'justiciable'. The reason the ECJ included acts of the Parliament within actions to annul despite the omission of the Parliament from Art 173 was to ensure that all legally binding acts were capable of judicial review. In *Group of the European Right v European Parliament* (1985), a decision by the President of the European Parliament declaring admissible a motion for the setting up of a Committee of Inquiry into the rise of fascism and racism was not capable of challenge.

Historical development of the European Parliament's powers

Examination questions frequently ask for an historical analysis of the development of the European Parliament's powers. It is important to keep certain key dates in mind.

1957. Founding Treaties give the Parliament the right to advise and be consulted, supervise the Commission and a small number of special powers.

1970/75. Budgetary Treaties give the Parliament power to reject draft in its entirety; final say on non-compulsory expenditure; propose amendments to compulsory expenditure.

1979. Direct elections. Not an increase in powers but an enhancement of the Parliament's moral authority which encouraged the Parliament to use existing draconian powers, ie rejection of draft budget to pressurise other institutions.

1986. Single European Act. Introduction of co-operation procedure. Co-decision for assent to new members and association agreements. *But* greater implementation powers for Commission.

1993. Treaty on European Union. More consultative powers. Co-operation procedure extended to new powers. Introduction of procedure referred to in Art 189b. Assent extended to new areas including legislative field. Power of veto over appointment of new Commissioners. 'Committees of Inquiry'. Right to 'request' proposals from Commission. Right of citizens of European Union to petition Parliament. Power to appoint Ombudsman. Consultative role in relation to the Foreign and Security and Justice and Home Affairs pillars of the Union.

The European Parliament started as a very weak body but has steadily been increasing its powers. Successive Treaties have augmented its powers with the possible exception of the Single European Act. Bieber *et al* 23 CML Rev 767 argues that although powers are increased by the Single European Act in some ways in particular in relation to the decision making process, the overall effect was neutral. As the Parliament has certain 'horizontal' powers over the whole of the Treaty they argued that the effect of the Treaty on the Parliament could only be assessed by considering changes in the powers of the other institutions. The increase in the implementing powers of the Commission affected the Parliament, firstly, as the committee system (whereby the Council retains some measure of control over implementing legislation) affects the Parliament in its supervisory capacity and secondly because the committee system weakens the Parliament's budgetary powers.

Increase in Parliament's powers

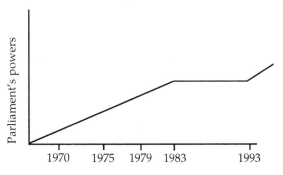

Budgetary powers are further weakened by the Single European Act as the total amounts for the technological and scientific framework programme are set by the Council after consulting the Parliament.

Although the Parliament gives the outward appearance of being like any other Parliament, the reality is quite different. Despite being the sole Community institution which has its members elected on a Euro-wide level, sovereignty still has a role to play. There are *pro rata* far fewer MEPs for the larger Member States than the smaller.

The Parliament has weak supervisory powers over the Council. The Council's decisions are taken in secret and its lack of accountability has lead to what has been called a 'democratic deficit' in the Community.

Court of Auditors

The Court of Auditors received the status of an institution by virtue of the Treaty on European Union.

Composition

There are 15 members appointed by the Council by the Council after consulting the European Parliament for renewable terms of six years. Members of the Court must have relevant auditing experience and must be independent. They may be removed from office by the ECJ if it is satisfied that the conditions and obligations of office are not met.

Role

The function of the Court of Auditors is to examine the revenue and expenditure of the Community and of bodies set up by the Community to ensure that all revenue has been received and all expenditure incurred in a lawful and regular manner and that all financial management has been sound. So it not only assesses the financial soundness of operations but also ensures that the means employed are the most economic and efficient. They will make spot checks amongst the Member States as well as the Community institutions. In the Member States the audit is carried out in liaison with the national audit bodies or national departments, who shall inform the Court of Auditors as to whether they intend to take part in the audit.

The institutions of the Community have the right to seek the opinion of the Court of Auditors on specific questions and the Court of Auditors can submit observations at any time on specific points.

The Court of Auditors produce an annual report which the institutions reply to.

The Courts

European Court of Justice

Under Art 164 the function of the ECJ is to ensure that in the interpretation and application of the Treaty the law is observed.

Composition
Judges and Advocates General. The ECJ consists of 15 judges and eight Advocates General. They must be independent and possess the qualifications required for the appointment to the highest judicial office in their respective countries or who are juriconsults of recognised competence. They are appointed by common accord of the governments of the Member States for a term of six years, expiring at intervals of three years, although they may be re-appointed. A judge can only be removed during his term if all the judges and Advocates General are agreed.

Every Member State has a judge on the Court. The intention is that the judge will represent the legal tradition of that particular Member State rather than represent the Member State itself. There is an uneven number of judges to prevent deadlock. The extra judge comes from one of the five larger states in alphabetical turn. The judges elect a President of the ECJ from among their number for a renewable term of three years.

The ECJ may sit in plenary session or in chambers which consist of three to five judges. The court sits in plenary session in all cases where an Institution or Member State so requests.

The Advocate General's position is curious to UK lawyers. The role was based on the *commissaire du gouvernement* in the French *Conseil d'Etat*. He has the same status as a judge and his duty is to present an impartial and reasoned opinion on the case, prior to the judges' deliberations. There is a slight resemblance to the *amicus curiae* in English law. An *amicus curiae* is a friend of the Court who gives the Court the benefit of his views on a question of law. A major difference between the two is that the Advocate General in contrast to the *amicus curiae* does not represent a particular interest and is completely independent. The opinion is usually but not always followed by the Court, and the opinions have no legal force. The Advocate General can only hope to influence the Court through the force of his judgment as he does not take part in the judges' deliberations. It has been suggested that as the ECJ was a court of both first and last instance when it was established the Advocate General's opinion provided an in-built appeal mechanism to the ECJ's deliberations.

Legal secretaries. All judges and Advocates General have two legal secretaries who will be qualified lawyers and help the judge or Advocate General prepare his case.

Registrar. The ECJ is served by a registry, headed by a Registrar. His functions are twofold:

- He is involved in the judicial function of the Court. Under his supervision a register is kept in which all pleadings and supporting documents are entered in the order in which they are lodged.

- The Registrar also plays a role in the internal administration of the Court, he is responsible for the administration, financial management and accounts of the Court.

Procedure

Procedure before the Court of Justice has four stages (although the second is often omitted):

- written proceedings;

- investigation or preparatory inquiry;

- oral proceedings;

- judgment.

Proceedings are commenced by written application. The application can be in one of 10 official or working languages of the Community. If the applicant is a Member State or individual the general rule is that the applicant has the choice of language. If the action is against the Member State the defendant chooses the language of the case. French is the working language of the Court.

The defendant serves a defence in reply to the application and it is possible for the applicant to serve a reply.

One of the judges is assigned the role of judge *rapporteur* and will study the papers relating to the case, which will also have been examined by the Advocate General assigned to the case. After close of pleadings the ECJ may decide that a preliminary inquiry is needed, although this is rare, the decision will be based on the judge *rapporteur's* preliminary report and the views of the Advocate General.

Prior to the oral hearing the judge *rapporteur* issues a report summarising the facts of the case and the parties' arguments. There are tight time limits on counsel during oral proceedings and the main speeches are not normally interrupted by questions. The Advocate General's opinion is also given orally but usually at a different time to the counsel's arguments.

Only one judgment is produced after the judge *rapporteur* has produced another report on the law relating to the case. Deliberations are in secret and the requirement to produce one judgment means that it is often anodyne where there has been disagreement between the judges, as it has to be sufficiently vague to promote agreement between all the judges. Judgments also tend to be bland for linguistic reasons.

The Court is bound to include in its judgment a decision as to costs. The usual rule is for the losing party to pay the winning party's costs but there can be exceptions such as staff cases, where the employer normally pays. Costs in preliminary references are normally reserved to the national court.

The Court can also grant legal aid. The Court will grant legal aid where it seems just and equitable to do so and it can be granted even where it it would not be available in national proceedings.

Jurisdiction
The jurisdiction of the ECJ has been conferred on it by Art 164, as follows:

- Actions against institutions, including actions for annulment (Art 173); actions for failure to act (Art 175); actions for damages (Arts 178 and 215) and at one time staff cases, which are now dealt with by the Court of First Instance.

- Preliminary rulings which are interlocutory references by a national court for a ruling on questions of interpretation of Treaties and secondary legislation and questions of validity of secondary legislation.

- Actions brought either by the Commission (Art 169) or a Member State (Art 170) against another Member State for failure to fulfil Community obligations.

- Since 1989 the ECJ has had an appellate jurisdiction and hears appeals from the Court of First Instance on points of law from undertakings which have been fined as a result of Commission Decisions relating to competition law.

- The Court can also give advisory opinions under Art 228 on an agreement between the European Union and third countries or international organisations.

Quasi-legislative role

One of the striking contrasts features of the ECJ is its approach to interpretation. The ECJ employs a purposive or teleological approach and interprets legislation in accordance with its aims and purposes. In this approach the Court is guided by the principle of *effet utile* or effectiveness and is constantly striving to ensure that their interpretation leads to a furthering of the integration process by ensuring that the European legal order functions more effectively. It is argued that the judges are not being creative at all; that they are precluded from performing a legislative function, as they are tied to the aims of the Treaties and are therefore limited in their policy choices, as a result. A problem with this analysis is that there is no unanimous agreement between the Member States as the form integration and consequently the policy choices should take.

The teleological approach has had several important consequences. Firstly, it has lead to a constitutionalisation of the founding Treaties. This constitution is said to rest on the 'twin pillars' of direct effect and supremacy. The principle of direct effect was established in *Van Gend en Loos* (1963) which held that a Treaty article could be relied on by an individual against a national government before a national court.

The principle of supremacy was established in *Costa v ENEL* (1964) and provides that where national law and EC law conflict, then EC law shall prevail.

The ECJ has defined the powers of the respective institutions and the competence of the Community. In *Commission v Council* 'ERTA' (1971) it was held that only the Community had competence to enter into an agreement with third countries when policy-making in a certain area has been handed over to the Community.

The principle of *effet utile* in combination with Art 5 under which Member States agree to fulfil their Community obligations, have been used by the ECJ to develop an interpretive obligation on Member States: *Von Colson und Kamman* (1986) and *Marleasing* (1989); and the safeguarding of rights through the availability of compensation in the event of the State breaching those rights: *Francovich* (1990).

The ECJ has also been involved in negative integration, ie the removal of barriers to trade. It has defined the obligations of the Member States in relation to free movement of goods, persons and capital.

Easson feels that the activist stage of the ECJ has come to an end and that now the general principles of the legal order are established then further developments will depend on the legislators. On the other hand, Ramussen feels that the ECJ has been unnecessarily activist in the past and will continue to be so in the future. Ramussen and Snyder see a danger in the ECJ's activist role as it lacks legitimacy to perform such a role and that there has been a lack of popular involvement in the development of the legal order.

Court of First Instance
The case load of the ECJ has increased dramatically since the inception of the Community. It can now take up to two years to receive a judgment. To help alleviate the workload, the Single European Act provided for the establishment of a Court of First Instance. The CFI was established by Council Decision 88/591 and began hearing cases in 1989.

The CFI consists of 15 judges and sits in chambers of three or five judges or occasionally in plenary session. There are no specially appointed Advocates General but a judge can be called upon to perform the function in a particular case. Article 168(a)(3) provides that to qualify as judges, '… members of [the] court shall be chosen from persons whose independence is beyond doubt and who possess the ability required for appointment to judicial office'. There is a President of the Court who is elected from amongst the judges. The CFI has its own Registry and the members of the Court have their own personal staff but otherwise all other services are provided by the staff of the ECJ and the CFI is 'attached' to the ECJ.

CAVENDISH LAWCARDS

Under Art 3 of the Decision, the CFI's jurisdiction was laid down, as follows:

- staff cases;
- actions brought by coal and steel undertakings under the ECSC Treaty;
- actions brought by natural and legal persons against a Community institution under Art 173(2) or Art 175(3) relating to the implementation of competition rules applicable to undertakings.

The competition and staff cases take up most of the CFI's time. Both types of case are fact based and were therefore thought suitable to transfer to a different court as they would be the most likely to alleviate workload. It had also been suggested that the CFI should also take over anti-dumping and subsidy cases, as they revolve around difficult factual questions. The question was left under Art 3(3) of the Council Decision to be left for two years. Indeed, it has always been envisaged that there will be further transfers of jurisdiction to the CFI and under a Treaty on European Union amendment the 'classes of action or proceeding' coming within the CFI's jurisdiction (with the exception of preliminary references) are left open, to be decided by the Council at the request of the ECJ.

It is possible to appeal a decision of the CFI to the ECJ, on points of law only, on three grounds:

- lack of competence of CFI;
- breach of procedure before the CFI which adversely affects the interests of the applicant;
- infringement of Community law by the CFI.

```
┌─────────────────────────┐
│     European Court      │
│           of            │
│        Justice          │
└─────────────────────────┘
            ▲
┌─────────────────────────┐
│ Appeals:                │
│ (i)   lack of competence;│
│ (ii)  breach of procedure;│
│ (iii) infringement of EC│
│       law.              │
└─────────────────────────┘
            ▲
┌─────────────────────────┐
│        Court            │
│          of             │
│     First Instance      │
└─────────────────────────┘
```

If the ECJ finds that an appeal is successful, it quashes the CFI's judgment. It can then give final judgment itself or refer the case back to the CFI for judgment.

Kennedy 14 ELRev 7 saw a danger that if a high proportion of CFI decisions ended in appeals, then there would be a minimal reduction in the ECJ's caseload. However, even of this were to occur then there would still be a saving in time for the ECJ as the facts have already been determined by the CFI, leaving the ECJ to apply the law.

Since the inception of the CFI there has been little reduction in the waiting time before the ECJ, as it coincided with an increase in cases.

Subsidiary bodies

Economic and Social Committee
The Economic and Social Committee represents all sectors of economic and social life, such as employers, trade unions, consumer groups and the professions. It is not an institution in the formal sense. It is an advisory committee and must be consulted by the Council or Commission when required. It is also entitled on its own initiative to prepare reports on specific fields.

The effectiveness of the Committee has been limited. Its opinions do not have to be followed and it tends to speak with a discordant voice as a result of its members representing conflicting interests and consequently taking opposing viewpoints.

Committee of Regions
The Treaty on European Union created a Committee of Regions which also acts in an advisory capacity. It is made up of representatives of 'regional and local bodies' so that decisions can be taken 'as closely as possible to the people'.

European Investment Bank
The European Investment Bank is the Union's long term lending bank and the regional development bank for Europe. It makes grants and loans for projects for developing poorer regions, modernising or converting undertakings or developing new activities within the common market, or projects of common interest to several Member States which are of such a size or nature they cannot be financed entirely by various sources available in the individual Member States.

4 Free movement of workers

Free movement of workers

Articles 48–51 of the EC Treaty provides for free movement of workers. Secondary legislation provides for detailed rules governing the right of entry on the territory of a Member State to carry out an economic activity; the right to remain in a Member State after having been employed there and the right to equality of access to and conditions of employment on the same basis as nationals of the host State. These rights are subject to exceptions contained in the Treaty concerning public policy, public safety and public health and an exemption in the case of public service.

Initially these rights were given to 'economically active' persons and their families. The purpose being to allow economically active persons the freedom to move around the Community so that 'workers' could move to the jobs and higher wages, in other parts of the Community. Free movement of workers helped serve an economic objective and could not be regarded as an objective in itself.

Gradually, it has been recognised that the free movement of workers includes a social dimension. The Preamble to Regulation 1612/68 states that free movement is a 'fundamental right' of workers.

In 1990 freedom of movement was extended to three categories of persons who were not economically active – students, retired persons and persons of independent means. The Single European Act exhibited a greater awareness of the 'social dimension' to freedom of movement and it has now become regarded as an objective in its own right.

The Treaty on European Union establishes a European citizenship, so that every person holding the nationality of a Member State is to be a citizen of the Union: Art 8(1). Every citizen of the Union will have the right to move and reside freely within the Territory of the Member States subject to the limitations and conditions laid down by the Treaty and by measures adopted to give it effect.

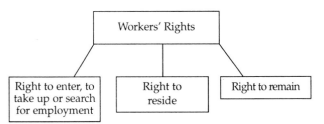

Article 48 is binding on individuals

Despite being addressed to Member States Art 48 is binding on individuals (*Walrave and Koch v Union Cycliste Internationale* (1974)). In *Bosman* (1995) rules of a national football association which limited the number of foreign nationals allowed to play and certain transfer rules breached Art 48.

Definition of a 'worker'

The term 'worker' is not defined in the Treaty. It is a Community concept and is not derived from national law. Community legislation and case law make it clear that a 'worker' is an employed person, irrespective of whether he performs managerial or manual functions.

The ECJ has given a wide definition to the term 'worker'. In *Levin v Staatssecretaris van Justitie* (1982) a chambermaid whose part-time earnings fell below the Dutch minimum wage and who supplemented these earnings with her own private income and had only taken the job to obtain the right to reside in the Netherlands did come within the Community definition of 'worker'.

The applicant in *Levin* had not been a charge on the State and had supplemented her low level of earnings by her own private means. However, a person is still classified as a 'worker' if their earnings need to be augmented by supplementary benefit (*Kempf v Staatssecretaris van Justitie* (1987)). A German resident in the Netherlands who had to have his part-time earnings boosted by supplementary benefit was still a 'worker'.

The definition of worker has been extended to trainees (*Lawrie Blum v Land Baden-Wurttemberg* (1987)). Where the applicant was a salaried trainee teacher who initially performed her duties under supervision but later independently came within the definition of 'worker', the ECJ said that the test for a 'worker' was whether someone was in genuine and effective employment and performing services for an employer under his direction and control in return for remuneration.

The meaning of 'genuine and effective employment' was further considered in *Steymann* (1988). A German national joined a Bhagwan community in the Netherlands. He was a qualified plumber and performed plumbing tasks for the community and also carried out general domestic tasks and assisted in their commercial activities. He was not given formal wages but was given board, lodging and pocket money.

The ECJ considered whether the work was genuine and effective and it was held that he a worker even though he did not receive any direct remuneration. The benefits which the Community gave to its members were considered to be an indirect advantage for the work that was performed.

The employment must be a 'real' job (*Bettray* (1989)). Dutch legislation created 'social employment'. Jobs were specially created for people to support them, rehabilitate them or increase their capacity for normal work. This was done through state-financed work associations, specially created for the purpose. Bettray was a German national living in Holland and was given 'social employment' as part of his treatment for drug addiction. He was receiving remuneration, but was not a 'worker', as the activities could not be regarded as genuine and effective. The job had been created to fit the applicant's capacity for work, as opposed to him being selected to do a particular job.

Dependants

Members of an immigrant worker's family have the right to reside in another Member State, even if they are not workers. The spouse and children of the worker can take up employment even if they are not EU nationals.

'Family' is defined in Art 1 Directive 68/360 as:

- the spouse of the worker;

- children, grandchildren and other descendants, provided they are either under 21 or dependent on the worker;

- parents, grandparents and other ascendants, provided they are dependent on the worker.

There are two types of rights. Independent immigration rights – available to workers, the self-employed, provider or recipient of services, student, retired persons or persons of independent means, citizens of the European Union – and there are also dependent immigration rights, which are granted to the family of a person with an independent right.

Dependent rights cannot exist without independent rights. Someone with an independent right to reside cannot lose that right as a result of someone else's actions but a person with a dependent right can lose their right to reside if the persons who has the independent right from whom they derive their rights, gives up their rights or if the relationship ends.

Article 10(3) Reg 1612/68 contains a provision that workers' family rights are dependent on the worker having adequate housing available. In *Commission v Germany* (1989) it was held that the housing only has to be adequate when the first family member arrives and the worker cannot be deported if it subsequently becomes inadequate.

A dependant family with parasitic rights obtain an independent right to remain if they were residing with a worker who dies and at the time of his death had acquired the right to remain in the host State or had resided continuously there for a period of two years.

The two-year residence requirement does not apply if the worker died from an accident at work or an occupational illness, nor does it apply if the surviving spouse was a national of the country concerned but lost this nationality on marriage: Art 3 Reg 1251/70 and Directive 75/34.

Co-habitees

A co-habitee's right to reside will depend on the laws of the host State: *Netherlands v Reed* (1986). Reed was a British citizen living in the Netherlands with her British boyfriend who had obtained a right to reside there. Reed argued that as her relationship equated with marriage, she had obtained a dependant right. The ECJ ruled that relationships outside marriage could not normally give dependant rights of residence. However, Reed was entitled to remain in Holland, as under Dutch immigration law a non-Dutch partner of a Dutch citizen had a right to reside. The Treaty contains a general principle of non-discrimination against Community nationals of other Member States, so on this basis Reed was entitled to reside.

The case does not create a general right of residence for co-habitees. Their rights will depend on the rules of the host State.

Separated and divorced spouses
A separated spouse retains a right to reside (*Diatta* (1985)). Although separated spouses still enjoy the status of a spouse, the situation could change if the parties actually divorce (*Secretary of State, ex p Sandhu* (1982)). The House of Lords held that an Indian man who divorced his German wife lost his right to reside. The case has been criticised for the House of Lords' failure to make a preliminary reference.

Dependant can be main breadwinner
In *Gul* a Cypriot doctor was married to a UK national and lived in Germany. He claimed that he was his wife's dependant, even though his wages were substantially in excess of hers. Nevertheless he was held to be a dependant.

Children of workers

Children of workers are entitled not only to education but also those rights which facilitate education, eg rights to grants (*Casagrande* Case 9/74).

Material scope

Article 48(3) provides workers with the right to enter and remain in another Member State for the purpose of employment and also to remain in that Member State after the employment has finished. These rights are in outline and have been supplemented by secondary legislation.

The right to enter

This right has been granted by Regulation 1612/68 and has been widely interpreted by the ECJ to include the right to enter in search of work (*Procureur du Roi v Royer* (1976)). Immigrant workers who enter another Member State in search of work can remain there for a reasonable time to appraise themselves of employment opportunities. If a reasonable amount of time has elapsed and the immigrant has failed to find work then the right to residence elapses. In *Immigration Appeal Tribunal, ex p Antonissen* (1991) the ECJ considered a 'six month rule' under UK immigration law which allowed immigrants six months to find work to be a reasonable length of time, but the rule operated too inflexibly and those with a genuine chance of employment at the end of the period, should not be deported.

Right to reside

A worker has a right to enter a Member State to find employment but the right to a residence permit is conditional on finding employment. The right to residence is a fundamental right, which is derived from the Treaty itself and not from secondary legislation.

To gain entry to a Member State only a passport or identity card is needed: Art 3 Directive 68/360.

Article 4(2) of Directive 68/360 provides workers shall be entitled to a residence permit. Rights of residence are not conditional on the permit it is simply proof of a right of residence (*Royer* (1976)).

A worker has an absolute right of entry under Community law so it is illegal to grant only limited leave to enter (*Pieck* (1980)).

A full residence permit is valid for at least five years and is automatically renewable. This means that persons entitled to it reside indefinitely, unless an event occurs which terminates the right.

It is not possible to deport someone on the grounds that they failed to comply with administrative requirements on immigration (*Watson and Belmann* (1976)) and failures to obtain a residence permit may be punished only if the penalties are 'comparable to those attaching to minor offences by nationals' and can never lead to imprisonment.

Temporary and seasonal workers. A temporary worker who works from three to 12 months in another Member State is entitled to a temporary residence permit in that State, to coincide with the expected period of employment: Art 6(3) Directive 68/360.

Those who work for less than three months or seasonal workers are entitled to reside in the State during the period of employment but are not entitled to a residence permit: Art 8 Directive 68/360.

The rights can be excluded to a long term or temporary worker and to a member of his family, on grounds of public policy, public security and public health.

Loss of Right to Reside

A temporary right to reside is lost when the purpose for which it was granted has been attained.

A full right to reside is of indefinite duration but can be lost in the following circumstances:

Departure. Absence for more than six months, other than for military service, can terminate a residence permit.

Unemployment. Article 7(1) Directive 360/68: a residence permit may not be withdrawn from a worker solely on the ground that he is no longer in employment either because he is temporarily incapable of work as a result of illness or accident or because he is involuntarily unemployed.

This implies that the right will be lost where the worker is voluntarily unemployed. The meaning of 'voluntary' unemployment is not clear. An obvious example is where someone gives up work of their own volition and makes no attempt to find new work.

A more difficult case would be where someone gives up work voluntarily but makes reasonable efforts to find a new job perhaps for an increase in pay or for a different type of work. Can a dismissed person who was sacked due to personal misconduct be regarded as voluntarily unemployed?

Article 7(2) Directive 68/360 provides that when a residence permit is renewed for the first time, the period of residence may be restricted to not less than 12 months if the worker has been involuntarily unemployed for more than 12 consecutive months. So in this limited example involuntary unemployment may lead to a loss to a right to reside.

In *Giangregorio v Secretary of State for the Home Department* (1983) it was held that the onus is on the worker to prove that he has been made involuntarily unemployed.

Access to employment/Equality of Treatment
There is a prohibition against discrimination on grounds of nationality which is laid down in general terms by Art 7 EC Treaty.

This has been held to be part of a wider principle of equality, which is a general principle of Community law (*Frilli v Belgium* (1972)). While equal treatment for migrant workers is expressly required by Art 48(2) EC Treaty.

These general rights have been fleshed out by secondary legislation. Articles 7–9 Reg 1612/68 and also the preamble to the Regulation require the abolition of 'any discrimination based on nationality between workers of Member States as regards employment, remuneration and other conditions of work and employment'.

Eligibility for employment (Articles 1–6)

Any national of a Member State has the right to take up activity as an employed person, and pursue such activity, in the territory of another Member State under the same conditions as nationals of that state: Art 1 Reg 1612/68.

It is not possible to restrict the number or allocate a certain percentage of foreign workers to be employed in an activity or area of activity: Art 4 Reg 1612/68.

States are entitled to permit the imposition of non-nationals conditions 'relating to linguistic knowledge required by reason of the nature of the post to be filled'. Art 3(1) Reg 1612/68. In practice this is one of the most important barriers to free movement. Workers are inhibited from moving to other States as they do not speak the language. Article 3(1) permits a requirement of linguistic knowledge where that is required for the post.

Language requirements can be imposed where there is an official policy to promote the language: *Groener v Minister for Education* (1989). Teachers in Irish schools are required to be proficient in the Irish language. Under the Irish constitution Irish is the first official language of Ireland and national law had a clear policy of maintaining and promoting the Irish language. The applicant was a Dutch woman who was barred from appointment as an art teacher at a college of marketing and design because she was unable to obtain the certificate. The Irish government claimed their action was justified on the basis of Art 3(1).

It was held that the EC Treaty does not prohibit the promotion by a Member State of its national language provided the measures taken to implement it are not disproportionate to the objective pursued and do not discriminate against the nationals of Member States. As teachers have a role in the promotion of Irish, a requirement that they have a knowledge of Irish was reasonable provided it was applied in a non-discriminatory manner and the level of knowledge to be attained must not be excessive in relation to the objective pursued.

Equality of Treatment (Articles 7–9)

Article 7(1) provides that workers must be treated equally in respect of any conditions of employment and work, in particular remuneration, dismissal and should he become unemployed, reinstatement or re-employment.

This covers both direct and indirect discrimination. In *Ugliola* (1969) a German employer took into account, for the purposes of seniority, employees' periods of national service in Germany. The applicant had done his national service in Italy and so it did not count. This was held to be discriminatory.

Social and tax advantages

Under Art 7(2) a migrant worker is entitled to the same 'social and tax advantages' as national workers.

The term 'social advantage' has been interpreted widely. In *Fiorcini v SNCF* (1975) it was held to include a special rail reduction card to parents of large families, even though that is a benefit which does not attach to contracts of employment.

A formula was developed for determining 'social or tax advantages' in *Ministère Public v Even* (1979) which were 'those which, whether or not linked to a contract of employment, are generally granted to national workers primarily because of their objective status as workers or by virtue of the mere fact of their residence on national territory'. Applying this test Belgium did not have to pay an early retirement pension payable to Belgian ex-soldiers who were in receipt of invalidity benefit to Belgian soldiers.

Social and tax advantages do, however, include benefits granted on a discretionary basis (*Reina* (1982)). An Italian couple were living in Germany, the husband was a 'worker' and they applied for a childbirth loan which was State-financed from the defendant bank. The loan was payable under German law to German nationals living in Germany. The bank argued that it was not a 'social advantage' under Art 7(2) as the loan had a political purpose as it was designed to increase the number of Germans. It was also a discretionary loan. It was also argued that the loan would be hard to recover from foreign nationals who returned home. The ECJ applying the *Even* formula held that it was a social advantage and covers benefits granted on a discretionary basis.

Similarly in *Castelli v ONPTS* (1984) an Italian, on being widowed, went to live with her son in Belgium. Applying the *Even* formula it was held that she was entitled to claim a guaranteed income paid to all old people in Belgium. She had a right to reside with her son and so was entitled to the same social and tax advantages as Belgian workers and ex-workers.

Rights of equality in the field of social and tax advantages does not apply to nationals of Member States who migrate in search of employment (*Centre Public de L'Aide Sociale de Courcelles v Lebon* (1987)). Lebon was a French national and was living and looking for work in Belgium and claimed benefit. It was held that the right to equality of treatment in field of social and tax advantages was only for the benefit of workers and not for those who migrate in search of employment.

Vocational training
Article 7(3) entitles workers to access, under same conditions as national workers, to training in vocational schools and retraining centres.

The extent to which this provision applied to education was considered by the ECJ in *Brown* Case 197/86 and *Lair* Case 39/86. Brown had obtained a place at Cambridge University to study engineering, and Lair had obtained a place at the University of Hanover to read languages. They claimed grants from the UK and German authorities respectively. Although Brown had dual French/British nationality he and his family had been domiciled in France for many years. He obtained sponsorship from Ferranti and worked for them in Scotland for 'eight months, which was intended as a preparation for his university studies. Lair had worked intermittently in Germany for five years with spells of involuntary unemployment.

The refusal was challenged under, Art 7(2) and Art 7(3) Reg 1612/68. Advocate General Slynn said that both courses constituted vocational training under Art 7(2). The question was whether Brown and Lair were 'workers'. He said that a distinction should be drawn between persons who migrate genuinely in capacity as workers and those who move to another State for other purposes, eg to gain work experience before studies begin. Only the former could invoke Arts 7(2) and 7(3). Although there was no minimum residence period, length of stay should be taken into account in assessing genuineness.

The Court took a different view: neither course constituted 'training in vocational schools' for the purpose of Art 7(3). The parties could only succeed under Art 7(2). Brown had only acquired the status of a worker because of his acceptance into university. In Lair's case the court drew a distinction between involuntary and voluntary employment. In the latter case, the applicant could only claim a grant for a course of work if there was a link between the studies and the previous work activity.

Trade union activities
Article 8 of Reg 1612/68 deals with discrimination in area of trade union activities.

Workers from other Member States have a right to equal treatment as regards trade union membership and the rights that go with it, eg right to vote. They must be eligible for appointment to workers' representative bodies in the undertaking.

Immigrant workers may, under Art 8, be excluded from taking part in the management of bodies governed by public law and holding an office governed by public law.

Housing
Article 9 Reg 1612/88 gives immigrant Community workers the right to equal treatment with regard to housing, including public housing. This would bar any rule precluding them from putting their name down for, eg council housing.

Exceptions

Article 48(3) allows an exception from the free movement of workers provisions where it is justified on grounds of public policy, public security or public health.

Article 48(3) is further fleshed out by Directive 64/221. Article 3 provides that measures taken on grounds of public policy or public security shall be based on the personal conduct of the individual concerned.

Meaning of 'public policy'

In *Van Duyn v Home Office* (1974) it was said that the concept of public policy is subject to control by Community institutions but the definition of public policy can vary from State to State.

In *Rutili v French Minister of the Interior* (1975) it was held that for the public policy exception to be invoked the threat must be genuine and serious. Restrictions are subject to the proportionality principle.

In *Bouchereau* (1977) the test was expressed as a genuine and sufficiently serious threat to the requirements of public policy affecting one of the fundamental principles of society.

Directive 64/221 lays down that public policy shall not be involved:

- 'to serve economic ends' (Art 2(2));

- previous criminal conviction shall not in themselves constitute grounds for taking measures (Art 3(2));

- expiry of the identity card or passport used by the person concerned to enter the host country and to obtain a residence permit shall not justify exclusion from the territory (Art 3(3)).

Meaning of 'personal conduct'

In *Van Duyn v Home Office* (1974) it was held that present association with a group or organisation could count towards personal conduct but that past association never could.

Van Duyn was a Dutch national, who was refused entry into the UK on grounds of public policy. She wished to take up employment with the Church of Scientology. Scientology was not illegal but was considered socially undesirable by the UK government. The refusal was based on personal conduct due to the applicant's association with the Scientology sect. The case was the first preliminary reference made by a court of the UK and the controversial result has been explained as an attempt by the ECJ to be accommodate the UK on its first reference.

The ECJ held that conduct does not have to be illegal to justify exclusion but must be socially harmful and administrative measures must have been taken to counteract activities.

The ECJ has after *Van Duyn* laid down much stricter tests. In *Bouchereau* (1977) a French national resident in the UK who had twice been convicted of drugs offences was deported from the UK. It was held that previous convictions should only be taken into account if there was a present threat to requirements of public policy but past conduct alone could constitute a threat if it was sufficiently grave.

In *Adoui and Cornuaille v Belgium* (1981) two French waitresses were working in a bar in Belgium but were also working as prostitutes. Prostitution was legal in Belgium but was discouraged. The Belgian authorities denied them a residence permit.

It was held that Member States could not deny residence to non-nationals because of conduct which when attributable to a State's own nationals, did not give rise to repressive measures or other genuine and effective measures to combat such conduct.

In *Bonsignore* (1975) an Italian living in Germany was deported after conviction of a criminal offence as a deterrent. It was held that a deportation order can only be made in connection with breaches of peace and public security which may be committed by the individual concerned.

Procedural rights

Article 9 Directive 64/221 provides that a person shall not be deported until an opinion has been received from a competent authority of the host country' before taking the decision. The competent authority must be separate from the authority taking the decision.

In *Santillo* (1979) a trial judge's recommendation to deport after a prison term was completed did amount to an 'opinion' under Art 9 but the opinion was not sufficiently proximate in time to the decision recommending deportation.

Public service exemption

Free movement of workers does not apply to public service under Art 48(4). This could be a very significant exemption but has been interpreted narrowly.

In *Commission v Belgium* (Re Public Employees) (1979) all posts in the 'public service' were limited to Belgian nationals. The Belgian government argued that jobs such as, eg nurses were within the public service. The ECJ disagreed held that it only applied to the exercise of official authority and it only applied to employees who were safeguarding the general interests of the State. Lower levels should be assimilated even though they could be barred promotion to higher posts. Such a bar would be legal.

5 EC sex equality legislation

Freedom from discrimination

At the outset it is important to distinguish between direct discrimination and indirect discrimination. Direct discrimination is where similar situations are treated differently or different situations are treated alike. This is always illegal. Indirect discrimination refers to neutral criteria which has a greater adverse effect on one sex compared to another. This is not an absolute principle and will be legal where it can be objectively justified.

Article 119

Direct effect of Article 119

In *Defrenne v Sabena (No 1)* (1971), the Advocate General indicated that Art 119 was capable of giving rise to rights to individuals.

This was confirmed by the Court in *Defrenne v Sabena (No 2)* (1975). However, the ECJ seemed to make a distinction between direct and indirect discrimination:

> within the whole area of application of Art 119 between, first, direct and overt discrimination which may be identified solely with the aid of the criteria based on equal work and equal pay referred to in [Art 119] and, secondly indirect and disguised discrimination which can be identified by reference to more explicit implementing [legislation].

It was also held that Art 119 had horizontal and vertical direct effect. The apparent argument that Art 119 only has direct effect insofar as the claim relates to direct discrimination has been interpreted as meaning that Art 119 cannot be relied on where the claim involves the assessment of criteria which cannot be taken into account by a court.

In the interests of legal certainty the effect of the judgment was limited, so that claims for backdated pay could only be made from the date of judgment, unless a claim had already been brought.

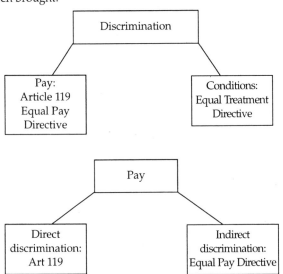

What is 'pay' for the purposes of Art 119?

Defrenne v Sabena (No 1) (1971), social security compulsory pension schemes which lack any element of agreement and apply to general categories of workers fall outside the meaning of 'pay' for the purposes of Art 119.

Criticism of *Defrenne (No 1)* test:

- discriminates between employees whose employers operate one form of pension scheme rather than another;

- operation of Art 119 may be dependent on the national organisation of pension schemes.

Contributions to a private occupational scheme which has 'contracted out' of a state scheme constitutes 'pay' within the meaning of Art 119 (*Worringham and Humphreys v Lloyds Bank Ltd* (1980)).

The first of a number of exceptions to *Defrenne (No 1)* was laid down in *Liefting v Academisch Ziekenhuis bij Universiteit van Amsterdam* (1984). Contributions to a state social security scheme affected the level of gross pay and therefore the level of other benefits did constitute 'pay' for the purpose of Art 119. It should be noted that the *Defrenne (No 1)* criteria were again affirmed in *Bilka-Kaufhaus GmbH v Karin Weber Von Hartz* (1984).

Barber v Guardian Royal Exchange Assurance Group (1988) again held that Art 119 applied to employers' contracted-out occupational pension schemes and to all redundancy payments. The inclusion of statutory redundancy payments was the latest exception to the *Defrenne (No 1)* principle and was confirmed with regard to 'top up' redundancy payments for workers aged 60–65 in *Commission v Belgium* (1993). Discrimination in pensionable ages in relation to occupational pension schemes was also held to be pay within Art 119 and therefore illegal.

The ruling in *Barber* was said not to be retroactive. However, there was ambiguity as to the meaning of this limitation of the temporal effect of the *Barber* judgment. An employee could not bring a claim 'with effect from a date prior to that of this judgment,' unless proceedings had been entered into prior to this date. Did this mean that the equal treatment principle applied only to benefits for periods after the date of judgment or to benefits for periods before judgment but payable afterwards? It was held in *Ten Oever v Stichting Bedrijfspensionenfonds voor Het Glazenwassers-en Schoonmaakbedrijf* (1991) that Art 119 could only be invoked for periods of employment after the date of the *Barber* judgment. A Protocol to the Treaty on European Union provides that the *Barber* judgment will only apply to periods of employment after the date of judgment.

Ten Oever was confirmed in *Neath v Hugh Steeper Ltd* (1991) which added that Art 119 could not be invoked to challenge the financial basis of pension rights accrued before 17 May 1990.

Further clarification of the *Barber* judgment was obtained in *Coloroll Pension Trustees Ltd v Russell* (1991). It was held that Art 119 applied to pensions paid under a trust, even though pension fund trustees are not parties to the employment relationship. Trustees are still under this obligation to observe Art 119, even if this is contrary to the trust deed. The equal treatment principle also applies to employers who have transferred their acquired rights from another pension fund which has not observed Art 119. This means that pension fund trustees may have to make good the cost of another company failing to comply with Art 119.

Article 119 does not apply to working conditions. Defrenne v SABENA (No 3) (1977): Art 119 does not stretch to equality of working conditions other than pay between men and women. Consequently, an attempt to use Art 119 as a means of ensuring equality of retirement ages under Art 119 failed.

Similarly in *Burton v British Railways Board* (1981), access to a voluntary early retirement redundancy scheme where women could apply earlier than men, is governed by the equal treatment directive and not by Art 119.

'Pay' includes non-contractual benefits. Benefits need only be granted in respect of employment to come within Art 119 and do have to arise from a contractual relationship: *Garland v British Rail Engineering Limited* (1982). Special travel facilities provided to retired male workers and their families which are not available to retired female employees and their families are 'pay' within Art 119.

Collective bargaining. In *Enderby v Frenchay Health Authority* (1992) it was held that where an occupation which was carried out predominately by women but where men performing different jobs but of equal value were paid more and the difference had been caused by separate collective bargaining processes, the onus is on the employer to show that the difference is objectively justified. The fact that the difference has been caused by separate collective bargaining processes cannot be sufficient objective justification. It was for national courts to decide whether difficulties in recruitment constituted objective justification.

Part-time workers. The cases relating to part-time workers have developed the law relating to indirect discrimination. Provisions which treat part-time workers adversely are not *prima facie* discriminatory as they affect both sexes. However, as part-time workers are predominantly women, such provisions will have a greater adverse impact on them.

In *Jenkins v Kingsgate (Clothing Productions) Ltd* (1980) it was held that a variation in pay between full-time and part-time workers does not breach Art 119, provided the hourly rates are applied without distinction based on sex and differences are 'objectively justified', this imported the concept of the employer's intention. It is rarely the employer's intention to discriminate but rather to gain a commercial advantage through the use of cheap labour. *Jenkins* was interpreted by English courts as meaning that if the employer's intention had been commercial advantage then that was objectively justified discrimination. This would have made it difficult for part-time workers to succeed under Art 119.

The effects of *Jenkins* were mitigated by *Bilka-Kaufhaus*; the ECJ held that it is for a national court to determine whether a policy is objectively justified but it was limited by the principle of proportionality, the employer has to show:

- that the policy meets a genuine need of the enterprise;
- was suitable for attaining the objective set; and
- was necessary for the purpose.

Statutory sick pay was held to come within Art 119 in *Rinner Kühn v FWW Spezial-Gebaudereinigung GmbH and Co* (1988). National legislation which allowed for differences between full- and part-time workers was illegal. The principle that legislation can be a source of indirect discrimination has enormous consequences for the UK, as can be seen by the case of *Secretary of State for Employment, ex p Equal Opportunities Commission* (1994) where the House of Lords held that provisions of the Sex Discrimination Act, which prevented part-time workers from claiming redundancy payments and compensation for unfair dismissal, were not objectively justified and consequently illegal.

Rinner Kuhn is also significant in that although the question of objective justification is left to national courts, the ECJ is prepared to set down limits as to what can constitute justification. In particular, it will look at the merits of justification arguments. So in *Rinner Kühn* the German government could not argue that part-time workers are less dependent on their earnings than full-time workers.

Significant guidance as to merits of objective justification arguments, in relation to small employers, was provided by the ECJ in a case under the Equal Treatment Directive in *Kirsammer-Hack v Sidal* (1991), when it was held that exclusion from employment protection for part-time employees of firms which had less than five employees was objectively justified on the ground that it lightened the administrative, financial and legal burdens on small firms.

Three recent German cases have also extended the rights of part-time workers. In *Kowalska v Freie und Hansestadt Hamburg* (1990) a provision of a collective agreement excluding part-time workers from severance pay infringed Art 119. The Court also held that the national court must amend indirectly discriminatory provisions of collective agreements as opposed to simply declaring them void.

In *Nimz v Freie und Hansestadt Hamburg* (1989) part-time workers had to work twice as long for reclassification to a higher grade than full-time workers. The ECJ held that in showing that experience is an objective factor which leads to improvement in performance, it would have to show that for that particular job additional experience was required in order to produce better performance.

Different problems arose in *Arbeiterwohlfahrt der Stadt Berlin v Botel* (1992) the applicant took paid leave in order to attend training classes. The length of the classes exceeded her working hours but she was only compensated for her normal working hours. This led to her being paid less than full-time workers for attending the same course. The ECJ said that the difference in pay could not be objectively justified as it would discourage part-time workers from undergoing training.

What is equal work?

Article 119 is not limited to situations where the man and the woman are contemporaneously employed (*Macarthys v Smith* (1979)). The applicant was paid less for the same job as her male predecessor had been paid. The ECJ also rejected the need for the adoption of a 'hypothetical male': the parallels could be drawn on the basis of 'concrete appraisals of work actually performed by employees of different sex within the establishment or service'.

'Equal work' enables applicants to compare themselves to other groups of workers who have had their work rated as inferior but still receive more pay (*Murphy v An Bord Telecom Eireann* (1987)).

Equal Pay Directive

Article 1 defines the principle of equal pay as being 'the same work or for work to which equal value is attributed.' This has been held as restating the equal pay principle in Art 119. So if a national court can identify discrimination solely by reference to Art 119, it will be directly effective. If discrimination can only be identified by additional criteria, reliance will be placed on the Directive (or its implementing provisions).

Initially, the UK implemented that equal pay was required where a man and woman were employed on 'like work' and 'work was rated as equivalent' on the basis of a job evaluation undertaken with the consent of an employer. This was held to be a breach of the directive in *Commission v UK* Case 61/81 as there had been a failure to provide a means whereby claims of equal value might be assessed in the absence of a job evaluation scheme. As a result the Equal Pay (Amendment) Regulations 1983 were passed and an industrial tribunal now has the power to have a report prepared to determine whether something is of equal value.

Commission v Denmark Case 143/83 allows for comparisons to be made with work of equal value in different establishments which are covered by the same collective agreement.

In *Rumler v Dato-Druck GmbH* (1987) a job evaluation scheme was challenged as the criteria it assessed included *inter alia* muscular effort. This was held not to be discriminatory so long as:

- the system as a whole precluded discrimination;
- the criteria used are objectively justified. In order to be classified as such they must:
  - o be appropriate to the tasks carried out;
  - o correspond to a genuine need of the undertaking.

In *Handels-OG Kontorfunktionaererernes Forbund I Danmark v Dansk Arbejdsgiverforening, ex p Danfoss* (1988) criteria such as 'flexibility' and 'seniority' could be taken into account in assessing pay. However, there were conditions attached to the ability to invoke 'flexibility'. If it meant that it was an assessment of the employee's work and women received less payment than men, then *prima facie* there would be discrimination and the onus would be on the employer to prove that the difference was objectively justified.

Danfoss (1988) is also interesting as it appears to accept 'seniority' as always being a reason to give more pay. This is hard to reconcile with *Nimz* where it was held that for 'seniority' to be taken into account it would have to be shown that longer experience lead to better performance in the particular job.

Equality of Treatment Directive

Scope of the directive
Male and female workers must receive equal treatment in access to employment, vocational training and promotion in respect of working conditions.

Equality of access
Equality of access to employment. This was considered in *Dekker v VJV-Centrum* (1988). The applicant's offer of employment was withdrawn when the employer discovered that she was pregnant. The employer argued that the intention had not been to discriminate, there had been financial reasons behind the move, as he would not have recovered the cost of the maternity benefit from the Dutch social fund. Nevertheless it was held to be a breach of the directive.

Ellis (1994) 31 CML Rev 43–75 argues that *Dekker* creates an extension to the idea of direct discrimination. The reason the applicant was not recruited was because she was pregnant; since only a woman can become pregnant, her sex was the cause of her failure to get the job. A causation test had been introduced to the concept of direct discrimination. Also, there was no actual male comparator in this case so it may signal a change of mind on the question of hypothetical comparators after *Macarthys v Smith*.

By contrast in *Handels-OG Kontorfunktionaerernes Forbund I Danmark v Dansk Arbejdsgiverforening, ex p Aldi Marked K/S* (1990) it was held that the applicant had not been unfairly dismissed for absences from work due to illness caused by a pregnancy two years earlier. The Court said that after maternity leave illness due to pregnancy should be treated like any other. The question then was whether she had suffered adverse treatment compared to a male employee.

Equality of access to vocational training. In *Danfoss* (1989) it was held that there was no discrimination where vocational training has been offered to a group of workers who are predominantly male, where there was an objective reason for offering to them. In this case, it was shown that the vocational training was necessary for the tasks which had been allotted to the predominantly male employees.

Collective agreements

Article 4 provides that provisions contrary to the equal treatment principle in collective agreements, internal rules of undertakings or rules governing the independent occupations and professions are to be nullified or amended by the courts.

In *Commission v UK* Case 165/82) it was held that this applies to non-legally binding agreements, as well as binding agreements.

Equality of working conditions

Article 5 provides for the application of the equal treatment principle to working conditions.

Conditions governing dismissal. Article 5 specifically states that working conditions include dismissal.

Access to a voluntary redundancy scheme comes within the meaning of dismissal for the purposes of Art 5: *Burton v British Railways Board* (1981). The applicant did not succeed in his claim as under Art 7(1) of the Social Security Directive it is possible to exclude from the equal treatment principle, the pensionable ages for men and women. Women could apply to the voluntary redundancy scheme aged 50, whereas men had to wait until 55, as the ages were linked to the statutory retirement ages for men and women it was held to be legal.

Article 7 does not apply where retirement age is calculated for 'other purposes', ie purposes other than eligibility for State pension: *Marshall v Southampton and South West Hampshire AHA (No 1) (1984); Beets-Proper v Landschot Bankers (1986)*. In both cases the applicants had been forced to retire at 60, whereas men could carry on until they were 65. The ages were linked to statutory retirement ages. The ECJ held that neither case concerned access to a pension scheme and was therefore prepared to draw a distinction between age limits for dismissal (which comes within Art 5) and age limits for pensions (which is caught by the exemption for pensionable ages).

Marshall (No 1) is also noteworthy as the ECJ held that directives could not have horizontal direct effect. (See Chapter 2.)

Adoption leave is not a working condition. In *Commission v Italy* Case 163/82 the Commission took enforcement proceedings in respect of an Italian law which provided for eligibility for women but not men for three months compulsory leave after a child under the age of six was adopted into the family. This was held to be legal by the ECJ, as they felt it was necessary to assimilate conditions of entry of an adopted child into the family to those of a newborn child. The judgment did not follow Advocate General Rozes' opinion. She argued that the paramount aim of adoption leave is to secure the emotional ties between the child and the adoptive family. This is a task which can be performed equally as well as by the father as the mother and therefore in the Advocate General's opinion it is a working condition.

Derogations from the equal treatment principle

As derogations depart from individual rights they must all be interpreted strictly (*Johnston v Chief Constable of the Royal Ulster Constabulary* (1984)). They are also subject to the principle of proportionality.

Where sex is a determining factor. Article 2(2) authorises Member States to exempt occupational activities 'for which the sex of the worker constitutes a determining factor'. This has been defined by the Commission to mean that there are 'objective reasons ... [why] the job can be carried out either only by a man or only by a woman'.

This article needs to be read in conjunction with Art 9(2) which requires Member States to periodically assess the occupational activities excluded in order to decide, in the light of social developments, whether there is justification for continuing with the exclusions concerned. This list is under the supervision of the Commission as Member States are required to submit a list of restricted occupations to them. Certain jobs require physical characteristics which determine that the job can only be done by one sex or the other, eg actor/actress, model, wet nurse, etc.

The derogation has operated in a wider context than this, however, to include jobs which social and cultural conditioning have resulted in the job being performed by one particular sex, eg midwives, firemen, etc. The function of Art 9 is to review social developments to assess whether attitudes have changed to a sufficient extent to enable certain occupational activities to be opened up to both sexes.

The significance of permitting social considerations into account is that they vary from State to State. Consequently, there is an element of discretion in the hands of a Member State as to what activities constitute excluded activities for the purpose of Art 9(2). This discretion is fettered, because the Art 9(2) list must be submitted to the Commission who are, therefore able to exercise supervision over it. Failure to produce a list will be a breach of the Directive (*Commission v Germany* Case 248/83).

Environment played a crucial part in the outcome of *Johnston*. The applicant had been refused a renewal of her contract as a member of the RUC full-time reserve and to be allowed training in the handling and use of firearms. The reasons given for the refusal were that it was necessary for safeguarding public security and to protect public safety and public order.

The ECJ held that regard had to be paid to the context in which an armed police force carries out its activities, which is determined by the environment. Arming women police officers in Northern Ireland places them under a greater risk of assassination than if they are left unarmed. It was therefore contrary to the interests of public safety to provide women officers with arms. On this basis, sex was a determining factor in the carrying out of certain police activities.

The ECJ said that even where a situation came within a derogation there was an obligation firstly, under Art 9(2) to periodically assess whether the derogation could still be maintained. Secondly, as this was a derogation from an individual right the principle of proportionality must be observed. There would have to be a balancing between the interests of equal treatment and public safety and it was for the national court to determine whether an action was proportionate or not.

This part of the ruling has been criticised by Prechal and Burrows in *Gender Discrimination Law of the European Community*. They felt that there was nothing in the evidence which suggested that armed women police offices were more likely to be assassinated than male officers. The Chief Constable had not, for example, asserted that armed women were more likely to provoke an armed response. By allowing questions of environment to be invoked, considerations other than biological differences and social considerations would be taken into account. Woman police officers have since been armed in Northern Ireland.

In *Commission v UK* Case 165/82 the Commission challenged the UK's exclusion under s 6(3) Sex Discrimination Act from the equal treatment principle of employment in a private household or small undertakings where the number of persons does not exceed five. The Commission also challenged the UK's prohibition on men applying for employment or training as midwives. The UK government argued that the exclusions came within Art 2(2).

The ECJ objected to the general nature of the domestic service and small business exceptions. Although there are particular jobs in both sectors which can only be performed by one particular sex, this does not justify exempting them entirely from the equal treatment principle. This was echoed in *Johnston* where it was again held that a woman could only be excluded from specific activities.

The exclusion relating to midwives was found to be legal. The ECJ referred to Art 9(2) and the need to constantly review excluded occupational activities in the light of social developments. It was held that the exclusion was appropriate given personal sensitivities, which existed at the date of judgment. These personal sensitivities were capable of making the sex a determining factor for the occupational activity. The judgment was contrary to Advocate General Roze's opinion, who thought that there was nothing in being a midwife itself which justified the exclusion and laid emphasis on the patient's right to choose the midwife she prefers. The UK has since allowed men to become midwives.

Recruitment problems arose in *Commission v France* Case 318/86. Separate recruitment took place for the French prison service. The Commission agreed that separate appointment to lower grades within the service was justified under Art 2(2), but objected to the fact that promotion to the higher grade of governor was discriminatory, as this role could be performed by a man or a woman. Yet a governor could only be appointed from the ranks of prison wardens for which there was separate recruitment. The ECJ held that there might be reasons for needing the experience of having been a warden in the prison before being appointed a governor and therefore the separate recruitment was legal.

Protection of women, in particular with regard to pregnancy and maternity. Article 2(3) provides for the second exception to the equal treatment principle whereby provisions are allowed which are for the protection of women, particularly with regard to pregnancy and maternity.

In *Hofmann v Barmer Ersatzkasse* (1983) questions relating to the interpretation of Art 2(3) arose. German legislation provided for two successive periods of maternity leave after the birth of a child. The first leave is compulsory and covers a period for eight weeks after childbirth, and the second leave is optional and covers the period from the end of the first leave until the child has reached the age of six months old. A sickness fund pays the mother a daily allowance during the period of the leave.

The applicant was a father of a baby and applied to the fund for the allowance in respect of the second period, while his girlfriend returned to work.

The authorities replied that the legislation specifically excluded the possibility of paternity leave.

The ECJ said that the purpose behind Art 2(3) was twofold:

- to protect the mother's biological condition during and after pregnancy until her physiological and mental functions return to normal;

- to protect the special relationship between mother and child by preventing that relationship being disturbed by multiple burdens.

On this basis the optional period of maternity leave fell within Art 2(3) as it was seeking to protect the mother. The ECJ said that it was within the discretion of the Member State as to the nature and the detailed implementation of protective measures. This was contrary to the Commission's wish that Art 2(3) be interpreted as strictly as possible.

The ECJ's decision has been criticised by Prechal and Burrows, on the following grounds:

- there is no indication as to the length of period needed to protect the mother's relationship with the child;

- too much discretion is left to the Member States, in the implementation of the rules protecting the mother;

- the aim of protecting the mother against multiplicity of burdens can be achieved by giving the optional leave to the father; as the mother would be relieved of domestic burdens. Protection against multiplicity of burdens can therefore be achieved by non discriminatory methods; and

- the Directive is not designed to organise family relationships and yet no choice is given in the division of work between home and family. The father must work and the mother must remain at home.

In *Johnston* it was again said that the purpose of Art 2(3) was to protect the biological condition of the mother and the mother's relationship with the child. It could not therefore be invoked where there is a general risk which is not specific to women, such as the threat to public order in Northern Ireland, where the risks would apply equally to men and women.

A stricter interpretation of Art 2(3) occurred in *Commission v France* Case 312/86. The French Labour Code allowed for the extension of maternity leave, reduced working hours, additional holidays at the start of the school year, allowances for a creche or babysitters, reduced retirement age and additional benefits for children of working mothers only.

This was held to contravene Art 2(3), special rights accorded to the mother after pregnancy and childbirth fall outside Art 2(3). It can be deduced from this case that 'maternity' only applies to the period immediately after childbirth and not to any longer period when the child may have started at school.

Positive discrimination. Article 2(4) provides for positive action on behalf of women. It has been interpreted strictly and the ECJ will only permit positive discrimination where it can be shown that inequalities actually exist: *Commission v France* Case 312/86. Measures are also only be of a temporary duration as they are subject to review under Art 9(2).

In *Kalanke v Freie Hanestadt Bremen* (1993) the ECJ ruled that national rules which guarantee women absolute and unconditional priority for appointment or promotion, go beyond equal opportunities and exceeds the positive action permitted under Art 2(4). The Commission has asserted that it only makes rigid quota systems illegal.

The concept of positive discrimination in Community law has been extended by its inclusion in the agreement annexed to the Social Protocol of the Treaty on European Union. Article 6(3) allows for measures of positive discrimination and does not require prior establishment of illegality and is not subject to Art 9(2) limitations.

Effective remedies

Starting with the cases of *Von Colson und Kammann v Land Nordrhein-Westfalen* (1984) and *Harz v Deutsche Tradax* (1983) it can be seen that the Directive requires real and effective sanctions, where there has been a breach of the equal treatment principle. Although there is no express provision to this effect in the Directive, Art 6 requires the Member States to introduce measures so that applicants who feel wronged by the failure to apply the equal treatment to them, can pursue their claims by judicial process. From this the ECJ has adduced the need for effective sanctions and said in its judgment in *Von Colson* that, 'it is impossible to establish real equality of opportunity without an appropriate system of sanctions'.

This has wider implications for Community law and the principle has been extended in *Francovich and Bonifaci v Italian Republic* (see Chapter 3).

More recently, the principle has been applied in relation to British legislation in *Marshall v Southampton and South West Hampshire Area Health Authority (No 2)* (1991). An arbitrary upper limit of £6,250 in the Sex Discrimination Act 1975 for the victim of discrimination was held to be contrary to Art 6 of the Equal Treatment Directive. The ECJ held that where financial compensation is the method of fulfilling the Directive's objectives it must enable the financial loss and damage actually suffered to be made good. In this respect the judgment differed from Advocate General Gerven's opinion which had stated that although the damages must be 'adequate' it did not have to be equal to the damage suffered. The court also said that an award of damages could not leave out matters such as 'effluxion of time' which might reduce the value of the award, therefore interest was payable on the damages. Finally, it was also held that for limited purposes Art 6 had direct effect. Where a Member State has been free to choose amongst a number of solutions which are suitable for achieving the objective of the Directive and has made its choice, then Art 6 may be relied on.

Procedural remedies. In addition to substantive remedies such as damages a case under the Social Security Directive: *Emmott v Minister of Social Welfare* (1990) held that it is also necessary to create effective procedural remedies. In that case it was held that limitation periods do not start to run until a Directive is properly implemented.

Interpretive obligation on Member States
It was said in *Von Colson* that Member States must interpret national legislation in accordance with the aims and purposes of the Directive, 'in so far as is possible'. Again this is a principle which has a wider application than equality law and has been extended in *Marleasing v La Commercial* (see Chapter 3).